BROKE, NOT BROKEN
Personal Finance for the Creative, Confused, Underpaid, and Overwhelmed

© This edition Microcosm Publishing 2021
First edition - 3,000 copies - June 8, 2021
ISBN 978-1-62106-684-2
This is Microcosm #445
Cover by Anna Jo Beck
Edited by Lydia Rogue

To join the ranks of high-class stores that feature Microcosm titles, talk to your local rep: In the U.S. **COMO** (Atlantic), **FUJII** (Midwest), **BOOK TRAVELERS WEST** (Pacific), **TURNAROUND** (Europe), **UTP/MANDA** (Canada), **NEW SOUTH** (Australia/New Zealand), **GPS** in Asia, Africa, India, South America, and other countries, or **FAIRE** and **GIFTS OF NATURE** in the gift trade.

For a catalog, write or visit:
Microcosm Publishing
2752 N Williams Ave.
Portland, OR 97227
https://microcosm.pub/broke

Did you know that you can buy our books directly from us at sliding scale rates? Support a small independent publisher and pay less than Amazon's price at **www.Microcosm.Pub**

Library of Congress Cataloging-in-Publication Data

Names: Beck, Anna Jo, author.
Title: Broke not broken : personal finance for the creative, confused, underpaid, and overwhelmed / Anna Jo Beck.
Description: [Portland] : Microcosm Publishing, [2021] | Summary: "A compassionate, friendly, and even fun book about personal finance for the overwhelmed. In a world with fewer and fewer economic guarantees, every bit of knowledge is powerful, so we can build the life we dream of, meet our basic needs, and develop a healthy relationship with money. For many of us, salaried work and even hourly wages aren't part of our financial picture; this book is for the self-employed, the entrepreneur, the creative, and the gig worker whose relationship with money isn't well covered by other books. Anna Jo Beck is your calm, friendly, and knowledgeable guide through the obstacle course of getting your funds, savings, spending, and debt in order. Hand-illustrated charts and worksheets mean you can start tackling your financial demons, building your safety net, and gaining confidence in your money and value right now"-- Provided by publisher.
Identifiers: LCCN 2020048656 | ISBN 9781621066842 (trade paperback)
Subjects: LCSH: Finance, Personal.
Classification: LCC HG179 .B355 2021 | DDC 332.024--dc23
LC record available at https://lccn.loc.gov/2020048656

MICROCOSM·PUBLISHING

MICROCOSM PUBLISHING is Portland's most diversified publishing house and distributor with a focus on the colorful, authentic, and empowering. Our books and zines have put your power in your hands since 1996, equipping readers to make positive changes in their lives and in the world around them. Microcosm emphasizes skill-building, showing hidden histories, and fostering creativity through challenging conventional publishing wisdom with books and bookettes about DIY skills, food, bicycling, gender, self-care, and social justice. What was once a distro and record label was started by Joe Biel in his bedroom and has become among the oldest independent publishing houses in Portland, OR. We are a politically moderate, centrist publisher in a world that has inched to the right for the past 80 years.

Global labor conditions are bad, and our roots in industrial Cleveland in the 70s and 80s made us appreciate the need to treat workers right. Therefore, our books are MADE IN THE USA.

CONTENTS

INTRODUCTION

This is a book for people who hate thinking about money.

There are so many personal finance books for people who enjoy thinking about money. There are books about stock picking, early retirement how-tos, even books for children about starting businesses. Many of these books are aimed at those who are obsessed with fine-tuning their strategies. But there aren't many books for people who can't bear gazing into the abyss of their financial choices, let alone their bank statements. I wrote this book because every book I read on personal finance seemed to be aimed at somebody else: the aspiring investor, the hapless debtor, the single-minded seeker of the American Dream. While each of these books brought me insight, none of them had exactly what I craved: a clear outline of the basic tenets of personal finance, without the frills and narrative angles of traditional prosperity. And most of all, a bit more cognisant of the current time and social standing many of us are in. The narratives of "pulling yourself up by your bootstraps" and "being poor is a state of mind" felt hollow and unhelpful as a queer woman with an immigrant spouse. I can appreciate that a positive spin may be inspirational to some, but in my experience dealing with finances can feel hard, and even unfair. Managing your finances is a long game that favors the people who already are in the know. It's commonplace for the topic of money to conjure feelings of confusion, anxiety, and fear. We absorb our emotional associations with money and how to handle it from our family, our upbringing, and our culture. For those of us who came of age around the Great Recession, the national narrative around money was one of insecurity and loss. Many from that generation are also saddled with one form of debt or another, with opportunities and wages not keeping pace. And that's what I think many books miss the mark on: they often operate with a homogenous set of conventional goals in mind and similarly assume that people are all at the same starting point, when actually our realities and abilities are vast and varied. Tips and tricks are great, but the path most books offered were limited to people who were building towards a future I didn't (or couldn't) aspire to: a big wedding, homeownership, traditional family. I wanted a book that acknowledged that thinking about

ny financial future brought up feelings of anger and
hopelessness while still giving a way forward to the life I
wanted to lead. This is that book.

I want to change how you think about money.

I wanted to write a book for people who have been
burned by money—people who have been trying to
follow their gut, but it keeps costing them. The margin
of error on healthy financial habits has become razor-
thin in the last few decades. Wages have stagnated, while
the cost of living increases rapidly. There are aspects of
our financial lives that are beyond our control, and that
is super frustrating. We should advocate for systemic
change, but in the meantime, one must learn to survive
and thrive within the current capitalist world order.

We will cover the fundamental building blocks of a low-
stress financial life. It sounds overly optimistic, but it is
possible, although it does take real work on your part.
I hope to guide you through this work of taking hold
of your finances in a way that's easy to understand and
implement. Truly, a lot of these concepts will seem

insultingly obvious, but the real trick is having patience and compassion for yourself while you work on rebuilding a foundation of habits that will improve your situation and outlook. Incredibly inspiring, I know, and not the silver bullet you were looking for, but it's true.

This book will sympathize with you, help you realize what matters most to you, and show you how to try to get it. I know money is hard, and all situations are different. There is no one-size-fits-all, right way to do money. We all go on our own journeys towards the individual life we want to lead, and we all have different starting points. Balancing the distinct ideas of what matters most to you, and equally important, what matters least to you, can have a massive effect on your life, and not just financially. This is a truly exciting and life-altering endeavor! I don't want to sound too grandiose, but when so many forces in our lives try and tell us what we should want, it's radical and empowering to decide for oneself what to seek and what to ignore.

This book will ask you to really examine, and actively choose, what is best for you and your financial situation. While I can't outline all the contingencies, I will offer advice on how to understand your current financials and how to build towards your future, no matter your starting point. Ideally, through this examination, you'll get a firm grasp on where you are in your current financial state and how to get to your goals, whether they be planning a cross-country trip, being debt-free, or a big wedding, if that's what you want! By seeing your situation clearly, it can change your original conception of money to one of utility instead of fear.

1

REFRAMING THOUGHTS

Before we dive into the numbers and budgeting, let's set the tone and consider the larger financial context we find ourselves in. "How does this help me, though?" you may grumble. Because you aren't a person figuring out a budget for yourself in a vacuum. History has weathered our position into the point we're at now, and hopefully this sheds some light on why the general aura around personal finance can feel both onerous and fatalistic.

What do you think of when you think of money?

Fat stacks of cash, expensive dinner tabs, your mountains of debt, etc. I'm going to ask you to set those initial thoughts aside and consider the larger and longer picture of society.

People have always needed goods and services, and as the world became more connected and technologically advanced, so did the methods of procuring said goods and services. To put it in a dense, run-on sentence: agrarian capitalism led to mercantilism, which gave way to industrial capitalism, an economic system based on the private ownership of the means of production and their operation for profit. Basically, we've been making advances over several centuries to more easily meet our basic needs: food, water, clothing, shelter. As technological advancements in farming made food production easier, other crafts and trades developed, adding variety and value to the marketplace.

It's only relatively recently, since the mid-1850s, that capitalism, as we see it today, starts to form. As a result of the industrial revolution, private enterprises such as manufacturing cars, household items, food, clothing, and other goods were able to be produced on a large scale—and quickly, expanded into a global market. Rapid population growth sustained the demand for those goods. By the 20th century, capitalism became the prevailing market force that runs the entire global economy.

Defenders of capitalism say that it spurs innovation through competition, allows productive people to thrive, decentralizes power, and creates prosperity and productivity. Critics argue that the power has already been centralized and solidified in those who have exploited both the environment and labor, and because those are the ones who prioritize profit over social good, it inevitably fosters inequality and corruption.

Safe to say, I'm a critic.

Capitalism in the previous century has shaped our social order. Mass production exceeded demands, so manufacturers resorted to planned obsolescence and advertising to manipulate consumers. We've been taught to believe that more is more, and social status hinges on just that. It's part of human nature to compare ourselves to others, and in a capitalist system, you can keep up with the Joneses with the swipe of a credit card. You worked hard, so now you can spend hard. Social cache used to be your lineage, your name, but now it's what you can buy.

Societal pressures aside, there's the very real struggle of the shift in wages versus cost of living in our current time, especially for Millennials and Gen Z compared with the previous generations, the boomers and gen X. Over the last 40 years, wages have basically stayed stagnant, while the cost of living has increased in many ways. College tuition continues to climb at quadruple the rate of inflation (soaring 1,375% since 1978). Average rental housing costs hit an all-time high of $1008 a month in 2019, climbing 20% faster than overall inflation between 1990 and 2016. Year after year, the annual Out of Reach report shows a family of four making minimum wage can't afford a two-bedroom apartment literally anywhere in the United States. Buying a home costs more than four times the median US income, while between 1980 and 1999, it was closer to three times. The annual healthcare costs for Americans in 1960 (adjusted for inflation) was $1325, whereas 2017's figure is $10,739. The most common reason for personal bankruptcy isn't online shopping but compounded medical bills. It's a topic of contention, but these are some of the forces that have shaped how entire generations view their financial lives.

And while it's true that overall the rapidly rising cost of education, housing, and healthcare affects us all, the inequality of opportunity compounds those costs among minorities.

For instance, you probably have heard of the gender wage gap. Women overall in 2019 still make only .79 cents for every dollar a man makes, but when you control for job title, years of experience, industry, and location, women are paid .98 cents for every dollar an equivalent man makes. What makes those two figures so different? For one, overall, women are less likely than men to hold high-level, high-paying jobs. Secondly, women of color experience additional barriers to getting fair pay and equal opportunity. At the start of their careers, Black and Hispanic women experience wider pay gaps than white women and are even less likely to advance to director and executive roles than white counterparts.

Employers present themselves as merit-based, but pay decisions do not reflect those espoused values. Comparatively, equal education is not valued the same between the sexes, let alone by race. Even in something as basic as asking for a raise, a 2018 PayScale survey found that while people of all races are equally likely to ask for a raise, women of color were 19% less likely to receive that raise than a white man. At 25% less likely, men of color fared even worse.

And more generally, Black and Hispanic American families are even further economically set back: the median wealth of Black and Hispanic families are $3,500 and $6,500, respectively, compared to the nearly $147,000 in wealth the median white family owns. Furthermore, 37% of Black families and 33% of Latino families have zero or negative wealth (meaning they owe more money than they own), compared to just 15.5% percent of white families.

That vast inequality of wealth also ripples through generations; one of the strongest determiners of your life chances are determined by your parent's socio-economic status. Upward mobility, aspiring to achieve economic success, no matter your background, used to be a cornerstone of "the American dream." For those born in 1940, that dream was achievable: there was a 90% likelihood that over time, children would out-earn their parents. Today, only half of all children earn more than their parents did. Nearly one-third of children with a father in the bottom quartile (as far as earnings) will grow up to earn in that same bottom quartile. Less than one-quarter of the children of manual workers become managerial/professional workers.

These factors of your family's race and wealth also affect your outcomes by means of what your educational opportunities are. Education is considered to be the most effective way to better your prospects in life, but there are large gaps in school quality, from kindergarten to college, that perpetuate inequality. A Department of Education study found that 45% of high-poverty schools received less state and local funding than other schools in their district typically received. Black and Hispanic students graduate high school at lower rates (78% and 80% respectively) compared to their white peers (at 89%), and that trend translates into generally lower college admissions for those minority groups as well. When looking at elite universities, the inequality of opportunity is enormous: children with parents in the top 1% (earning at least $422K annually) are 77 times more likely to attend an elite college than those with parents in the bottom 20% (earning less than $25K annually).

And, of course, that brings us to the adage that the rich get richer, and the poor get poorer, which has proven true, especially in our current era. The concept behind the cliche is that newly created wealth is concentrated with those who were already wealthy to begin with, giving them leverage to create even more wealth. A devastating contemporary example of this is that the wealthiest 1% of Americans captured 95% of financial growth since 2009 (post-financial crisis), while in that time, the bottom 90% of the population lost wealth. Oxfam found in 2014 that the bottom half of the world's population, that's 3.9 billion people, collectively owned the same amount as the richest 85 people in the world; three years later, that figure dropped to 8. Eight men now own more wealth than half of humanity combined. This is not only alarming for an individual's prospects, but societally: the wealthy have sway over government policymaking, and they use that to create further advantages for their industries and themselves, enshrined in law, effectively diminishing our democratic equality. Instead of a fair and equal society, we have rapidly been separated by economic and political power, which heightens social tensions and ultimately edges us closer to societal breakdown.

All this is to say:

It is not wrong to be overwhelmed and frustrated by money and the oppressive injustice that surrounds it.

Reckoning with your wider financial context is important; it's acknowledging the situation that you were born into. Inequality and racism are still rampant; by random chance of birth, we are each given a set of wildly unfair advantages and disadvantages. The conditions of inequality are incredibly unjust, but you can not change them by your own force of will.

At a certain point, you need to know how to best take care of yourself as an individual amidst these injustices. This is where learning about how to manage your personal finances comes in. The basics within this book will prepare you for surviving (and ideally, thriving) in this modern era.

In day-to-day life, there are so many social and behavioral forces that form how we think about money, and it leaves most feeling stressed and anxious. And it's completely valid and well-founded to feel that way. The tried and true financial playbook of the past (go to college, get a job, a spouse, and save for a 20% down payment on a home, work in the same job for 40 years, and retire in comfort) simply isn't feasible or desirable for everyone anymore. You need to make your own financial path, using updated tools and expectations.

Learning these basic tactics will not only help you on the road to financial security, but they have really amazing by-products: you learn more about yourself, your habits, your motivations, and your goals. These are your armor and shield against market and societal forces; know thyself and to thyself be true. One of my favorite pieces of personal finance advice is from writer Ramit Sethi: "Spend extravagantly on the things you love, and cut costs mercilessly on the things you don't." I'll get into this philosophy more (because of course no one loves paying the electric bill, but here we are, paying the electric bill), but it cuts to the core of it: you need to know what you love and what you do not love, and you'll need to tune out the noise of commercials, coworkers, and capitalism to hear what your heart has to say. But it makes this whole effort worth it: to live a secure life, filled with the things and experiences you, specifically you, love. I'm not going to say it will be quick, easy, or guaranteed, but isn't a life of your own design worth striving for?

And one last note before we go into the nitty gritty:

You will make mistakes.

You will probably make choices that don't turn out as you thought. Life will throw unexpected turns at you (and maybe you've already found yourself in some tough situations). As you read this book, you may see some tough choices rise to the surface or some regrettable past decisions present themselves.

It is of the utmost importance to learn to forgive yourself.

Even the most educated finance gurus have made mistakes. Life also throws us unexpected wrenches all the time. What puts the financially savvy on the right path is not a perfect track record but that they have identified the misstep, and taken a step towards a better solution. No matter how dire the situation feels, so long as you've made a plan to recover, you're doing better than before. Taking a step towards better is infinitely more valuable than trying to be perfect (or doing nothing at all). And once you've put a plan in place, there's the task of coping with any lingering feelings like worry, fear, guilt, and uncertainty. Cultivating compassion is key here.

This also extends further than the unexpectedly expensive bar tab; some financial missteps will take years to recover from. Dealing with student debt or experiencing a costly medical emergency can be long hauls to ride out. But so long as you're working towards a better situation, try to give yourself a bit of credit and take a bit of pride in that you're doing the best you can. Nurture a sense of goodwill toward yourself for facing this tough situation.

The only way out is through.

All these conditions have culminated to make us think that money is hard and stressful, which it absolutely can be, but most importantly, it is powerful. It's a medium—a way of exchanging our time and our energy for things we need to survive as well as bring meaning to our lives. While money (and lack thereof) can cause unending tragedy, a good financial strategy is essential to striving for our ideal lives. The key is being able to slowly grow your money confidence, and put it to work with patience and compassion. I promise you; it is worth it.

2

THE FUNDAMENTALS

These days, it's not always a given you'll be able to "live within your means." Life isn't a straight line. It's often a dance between striving for opportunity and cascading misfortunes. To create stability, you have two levers of personal finance: income and expenses. Ideally, you have command over these levers, but sometimes you don't, with outside forces making them go haywire beyond your control. The best you can do is know how to pivot and adjust these levers to your advantage: maximize income and minimize expenses, and ideally find some peace in it all.

First Lever: Maximize income

Maximizing income is without a doubt a difficult pursuit. Heck, even just getting a job is difficult. But where you can only decrease your spending to a point, the potential to increase your income theoretically has no limit. To be fair, it isn't always easy to increase your income, and it's often a long pursuit.

The most upfront way of maximizing income is asking for a raise at your current job. Another is to add income through a second job or side hustle. Sometimes finding a new employer is the quickest way to increase your income by negotiating a higher pay rate before you sign on officially. In a longer-term plan, you could consider pursuing a higher-paying job in a different field, potentially also seeking out further education or an apprenticeship. Maybe you need to sell some of your belongings. None of these are easy, but they are considerable.

I know this sounds daunting, and I completely agree. It is unconscionable how difficult it is to meaningfully increase your income. It is intolerable that the federal minimum wage hasn't increased since 2009 and that we are at Gilded Age levels of inequality, while productivity has steadily increased since the '70s. 43% of Americans are poor, or one emergency away from being poor. I do not say this to discourage you. I say this to underline just how dire our circumstances are to begin with. The best we can do, without meaningful political access to change the system, is try to strategically play the game as an individual.

Second Lever: Minimize expenses

Spending money is often thought of as the easier of the two levers to control. You, after all, have a great degree of control over what you buy.

There are strategies of how to minimize expenses: differentiating wants from needs is a big one, but it's hardly black and white. For instance, new clothing may be generally considered a "want", something nice to have. However, if you're faced with purchasing new clothes to comply with an employer's dress code, that nudges it towards the "need" end, as it enables you to keep your job and earn income.

The goal is not to eradicate all "wants" from your spending and only spend on "needs"; life is honestly too short to deprive yourself of all pleasures and that ultimately isn't sustainable. We'll get into striking your personal balance between wants and needs in chapter six.

But it also bears mentioning that you can only minimize your expenses so much, despite the illusion of control. You can choose your housing, healthcare, and education, but the general range in cost of these has ballooned disproportionately to income. While you certainly can be strategic in these choices, they are much harder to negotiate, and take up a larger chunk of your budget than more discretionary purchases.

Additionally, some expenses aren't expected: medical emergencies, car repairs, and other burdens. This is where having money tucked away from saving comes in. It is still worth noting that minimizing expenses is the goal, but isn't going to be the reality all the time.

My last "fundamental" is a bit sentimental, but something that's helped me along the way:

Try to feel gratitude towards everything you spend on, especially the unsexy "needs."

You may think you value and appreciate everything you buy (why else would you have bought it?), but it's worth making mental space to appreciate what you own and be considerate of the things that you buy. Living in our consumerist society can make contentment seem like it's just a few purchases away. Money can buy so many conveniences, but "retail therapy" on its own rarely produces lasting happiness. Savor the things you have that you love and the items that bring convenience and joy to your life. My backpack holds my things from place to place, keeps the rain out, and has a particularly wonderful texture of soft rubber that I enjoy immensely. An external hard drive, while normally inert, holds pictures from the previous decades of my life, promising to be on hand should my computer die. Trinkets from travels remind me of the wonderful places I've been. In many ways, gratitude has a grounding component and can enrich our lives further than consumer goods alone can.

But while things that give us good memories and convenience are easy to appreciate, it can be harder to appreciate things that you begrudgingly have to fork over money for. No one really likes paying for some of what we'd call needs.

When I first began organizing my financial life, it was disheartening to look at where most of my money went: a huge chunk to a slimy landlord, utilities I felt gouged by each month, the student loan debt payment that felt like throwing a teacup of water on a roaring wildfire. It was easy to appreciate the purchases that brought me joy: a pair of concert tickets to surprise my partner, toys that my dog loves, a haircut that changed my life—all money happily spent. But paying for dentist appointments caused me to grimace and huff. Even scrounging for laundry quarters felt like a burden.

I carried on like this for years: easily demonizing my needs and effortlessly loving my wants. Until my partner got sick, very sick, cancer sick. At first, I was both enraged and scared about how much everything would cost, and how little control we had on the services rendered. It was completely overwhelming to manage finances alongside caring for someone you love who's fallen ill. Luckily, my spouse's health improved and the bills were mercifully manageable. Even though they were still pretty hefty payments, I started to feel a small sense of appreciation for the money paid to the radiologists, surgeons, and pharmacists who helped my husband recover. It sparked a radical shift in my thinking that freed me from seeing every payment as a hardship, to a repayment of a service we needed to survive. Do I still see huge flaws in healthcare billing? You bet! It still sparks fury in me. However, at a certain point, I negotiated the best rates I could, and I needed to find a way to allow myself to be at peace, even with a maelstrom of bills around me. Knowing that I made my best effort and that, in a larger way, my partner's health was worth the price, brought that peace.

This sense of peace crept into how I feel about the other large expenses in my life: my rent is a bit high, but we love our little house in the city with skylights and easy access to public transit. Insurance payments (while still unacceptably high and debatably inhumane) offer us protection from even worse outcomes. After a good faith effort to find the best price for your budget and your needs, there comes a point where you've done your best, and hopefully that can give you a chance to be grateful and proud that you've created a functional life for yourself.

Before we go further, let's familiarize ourselves with some basic vocabulary.

The financial tool set

(feel free to skip ahead if you're familiar with the bolded concepts)

Cash: We all know this stuff. It's money! It's paper! (well, technically fabric, but a very paper-like fabric). It's anonymous! It's easy! And while it's nice to have some on hand, it's much more secure to store it in a bank in a **checking account.** Checking accounts are available at most local and nationwide banks, and even online banks without physical locations. A checking account is the simplest bank account that retains your cash securely (backed by the federal government). They originally provided you blank paper **checks** in order to write out payments from that account to pay for things. In our modern era, checking accounts come with a more convenient **debit card** to swipe for purchases directly from your account, or withdraw (to take out) physical cash from your account via an ATM. Usually, checking accounts are free to open and maintain, although it's becoming more popular for banks to require a minimum balance to avoid a monthly fee. Many employers also offer to do a **direct deposit** of your paycheck, so that instead of having to take a check to the bank to be redeemed for cash, it is directly deposited (obviously, right?) into your checking account.

You could also deposit or transfer your money at the bank into a **savings account.** This type of account is great for being able to set money aside from your normal checking account to better visualize your progress towards savings goals. It also separates the funds, making them ever so slightly harder to access (usually a day or so for a transfer to go though, but some accounts are instantly transferable) Savings accounts also typically have the minor benefit of a small **interest rate,** a percentage that the bank pays directly into the account for the privilege of holding your money. You can also have more than one savings account, say if you wanted to have different accounts for different goals, for example a car, vacation, or an **emergency fund.** What's an emergency fund? Beyond an imposing name, it's just a savings account specifically meant to be a cushion should something unexpected happen such as job loss or illness. (I'll talk about emergency funds more in chapter 5).

While they look very similar, a debit card is very different from a **credit card**. A credit card acts as a payment method in which the credit card company pays for items for you in advance, and then you repay the credit card company, typically in a lump sum on a monthly basis. Many credit cards offer a variety of benefits to their users: consumer protections, points redeemable towards future purchases, extended warranties. However, there is a nasty catch—if you aren't able to repay the entire balance in a given month, the credit card company tacks on a fee that is a certain percentage (**APR**, or annual percentage rate) of what you've spent, currently averaging around 16%. When you don't pay off your full balance of your credit card, that is credit card debt, which can add up quickly. There's more details on credit cards in chapter 5, but that's the quick outline.

And these are just the beginning! Think of these as the hammers and screwdrivers of your tool set—pretty straightforward on their uses. We'll expand into more specialized tools as we go along, but it's enough to get started.

3

EARNING MONEY

On the road to adulthood, many of us have milestones that allow us to be further independent: potentially receiving an allowance, going on our first job interviews, getting our first paychecks. All of these have a central theme of earning money.

Earning money is a necessity to being able to survive in the current world, but it also can help you attain the things you want from this life. On the overly glamorized end, an entire generation was encouraged to pursue a career that aligns with their passions. On the grim end, having an income is needed to maintain being fed, clothed, and sheltered, as well as to prove that you are a "contributing member of society." I believe the truth of most people's situations lies in between those two extremes of what an income represents. There's more to life than just getting by, but there's also unrealistic expectations on what fulfilling work is.

Distinguish between hobbies, jobs, careers, and vocation.

Every child can answer the question: What do you want to be when you grow up? It's a question that seems so harmless, but when you consider it beyond a topic of small talk with a child, it's a relentless question in our society. There's a lot of myths and expectations around what people "do" and I wanted to take a moment to say: *You should not be defined as a person by the means in which you generate income.*

I'm of the millennial generation that was encouraged to "chase their dreams" and "follow their passions", and this can be really discouraging to the 52% of Americans who report being unhappy at work. There's an inherent belief that you should aspire to have your passions directly generate meaningful income over a long career, and while possible for some, it's helpful to realize that it's not possible for everyone and isn't the only path.

Elizabeth Gilbert has a fantastic theory of the differences between jobs, careers, hobbies, and vocations. These words are often used interchangeably, but can and should have their own distinct meanings:

Job

The only thing you actually have to have on this list. It's a form of employment in order to make money to be able to provide for yourself. It doesn't have to fulfill you, you don't have to like it, you just have to be able to complete the given tasks in order to be paid. If you don't mind the work, amazing. If it's an abusive workplace, try to get a different job, being miserable at a job is not worth it. Just recognize that your job is not your entire life, just a route to attaining income.

Career

A career is a job or job track that you are passionate about and that you love. You are willing to make sacrifices and invest both time and energy into progressing in this field. You should absolutely love your career or not have one. If you hate your career, that's a problem, just get a job. A career is an all consuming commitment to work in the field above and beyond a job, that you do because you love it. It is not required of you to have a career, it is required for you to have an income (via a job). If you are in a career (a position where you are expected to love and be passionate for the work) that you hate, it may be time to consider other options, as you may be overworking yourself needlessly to an extent.

Hobby

Something you do purely for pleasure or entertainment, there are absolutely no stakes: it doesn't provide income or fame. It can be a passing fancy or a lifelong enjoyment. It's not something you have to do, but it's a fun thing to do. Karaoke, gardening, watching movies, reading, and cooking can be examples.

Vocation

This is the tiny (sometimes loud) voice inside of you that drives you to do or create something. It is a calling; it's the highest possible pursuit you can have. Unlike a job or a career, no one can give it to you and no one can take it from you. For many people it's a creative pursuit: writing, art, music, but it can also be volunteering or a spiritual/religious calling. You are internally driven to do this, but in the meantime, you still need an income. This drive can lead into a job or a career, but there are no guarantees that it will. In fact, pursuing a career alongside nurturing a separate vocation can be counterproductive; you may not have time and energy for both. You do the vocation because you feel compelled to. Not everyone has a vocation, and that's okay. Some people find them through hobbies, but a vocation is a seperate desire that is unstoppable.

The work you do to generate income can be meaningful to your soul, or it can just be a job—both are valid. The amount of money you make doesn't say anything about your worth as a person. Where your income comes from isn't who you are; it's your actions and beliefs that determine what kind of person you are. These are essential truths, even if others choose to judge along these lines. We live in an unjust, unequal world, but everyone has the right to dignity.

Earning an Income

The common way to earn money is compensation for work rendered for an employer. You are given an agreed upon rate for a set of performed tasks over an agreed upon range of time. Again, you don't have to love it, but ideally it's tolerable and pays on time.

Depending on your field of employment, as you gain experience, the more valuable your time as a worker can become. Typically, to increase your income you: attain employment, gain experience, then seek promotions or new opportunities with other employers. There are alternatives to receiving a typical paycheck: you can freelance your skills, work "gig economy jobs" like Uber, PostMates, and the like, or start your own business. As one ages, working becomes more of a burden, and other potential income streams become available: pensions, social security, and investment returns. All this to say: there are many forms of income and it will change throughout your lifetime.

It's a milestone of adulthood to land your first job, fill out that W2, and get that first paycheck from an employer. It's a moment of empowerment to receive your first bit of formal compensation for your hard work, but a single glance at the other numbers on your paystub can be deflating—those dreaded taxes, taken out before you could even see the money. I couldn't go far into income without discussing taxes. I know it seems off topic, but taxes come hand in hand with income, and it's worth having a general idea of how they work.

Our government collects several taxes on income to pay for things deemed socially necessary. Taxes commonly taken out of income are a federal tax (ranged and bracketed by salary, but roughly 10%-25%), a state tax (ranges by state, but roughly 5%), a social security tax (~6%), and a medicare tax (~1.5%). I could get much deeper into how taxes work, but for now, let's just accept that as fact, no matter what type of work you attain, taxes are unavoidable.

In addition, if your employer offers benefits that you opt into such as health insurance, 401k, or transit assistance, these would be deducted from your pay before taxes. It's great, because you effectively lower the amount that's taxed, however, it does mean you take a little less home in cash on the paycheck.

I bring up these tax percentages and other deductions to say that there is a meaningful difference to your hourly rate of payment (gross rate) and the amount of payment you receive after these tax and other deductions (net rate).

It's really valuable to know how much you actually take home per hour after taxes and deductions; it is essential to building your personalized financial life and outlook. It's also super simple to figure out.

If you have employment with a paycheck, you can figure this out now. Look at your last pay stub and take that net income amount (the amount that was actually deposited in the bank or on your cashed check) and write it below. Also on your pay stub should be the total hours you worked for that pay period. Write that sum in below as well. If you're paid salary, add up the hours you worked in that pay period (ex: 2 weeks, 40 hours per week = 80 hours). If you have multiple income streams, add together your take home income total as well as hours worked total for a general idea.

\$____ : Your net income

$$\div$$

____: The hours you've worked for that net income

\$____ per hour, aka hourly "take home" wage
You can also think of it as "this is the amount of money I receive in cash per hour of work." Formally, this is called

"net rate" in accounting, but it's commonly known as "take home" wage.

I encourage you to plug in your own numbers, but if you'd rather, feel free to just focus on the example below. For our example, we'll be using the median hourly wage for Americans as of May 2018, which is $18.58. Note: The "median" is the "middle" figure in the list of numbers. It's different from an "average" you're used to, where you add up all the numbers and then divide by the quantity of numbers in a set. The median in this example means half of working Americans make above this amount, and half make below, according to the Bureau of Labor Statistics. If you aren't currently making as much as this example, that's normal; half of working Americans are making less than this rate.

The amount of taxes and deductions out of your paycheck will vary by state and situation (if you have health insurance, the amount of money you make to begin with, etc.). For this example, let's say you are working full time, are paid weekly, you don't have insurance through your employer, and live in Chicago, IL:

In our example, the difference between the total earned, $743, and the actual money received, $584, after taxes are deducted, is a roughly 20% reduction. With these figures, you can now find your hourly "take home" wage:

$584 : Your net income

÷

40: The hours you've worked for that net income

$14.60 per hour, aka hourly "take home" wage

Knowing this figure is the start of your individual financial journey. Once you've calculated it, it is simply a really straightforward way to think about how you are actually compensated for your time, and it can inform all sorts of financial choices. It can be a helpful measuring stick to keep in mind when you're moving through the world as a consumer: Is this $14.60 movie ticket worth the hour I spent to earn it? Is this $29.20 pair of headphones worth the 2 hours I worked for it? Sometimes your answer may be yes, and that's great! It can also be humbling: the average rental apartment is $1008 a month, or and in our example, that's 70 hours worth of work. Your "take home" wage is a key barometer for deciding and planning on financial matters.

Knowing your "take home" wage is a great start on your individual path, and good enough to skip on to the conclusion of this chapter. However, it's also impactful to

EARNINGS	rate	hours	this period		EARNINGS STATEMENT	
	18.58	40.00	743.20			
	GROSS PAY		$743.20		PERIOD BEGINNING:	03/22/2020
					PERIOD ENDING:	03/28/2020
DEDUCTIONS	Statutory				PAY DATE:	03/29/2020
	FEDERAL INCOME TAX (9.01%)		-66.96			
	SOCIAL SECURITY TAX (6.20%)		-46.08			
	MEDICARE TAX (1.45%)		-10.78			
	IL STATE INCOME TAX (4.67%)		-34.71			
	NET PAY		$584.67			

THE TINY TIP OF YOUR ACTUAL CHECK AFTER TEARING IT OFF TO CASH IT.

consider not only the hours you are on the job, but also the expenses you have to maintain your employment and time spent on your commute. If that feels overwhelming, skip the following two exercises, and maybe come back later.

Work Expenses

There are usually additional expenses related to maintaining employment. Perhaps you have to commute to your job; there are costs to owning a car, taking public transit, and even biking. You may need to purchase your own professional clothes or uniforms. There's also potentially work-related meals and other expenses you pay out of pocket. If you're a freelancer, you might pay for a studio space or rent equipment. Estimate how much you spend in a given month on expenses that directly contribute to your success in your employment:

- **$___: Transportation**
  (car expenses such as gas, monthly payment, insurance, tolls; public transit, bike maintenance, etc.)

- **$___: Professional appearance**
  (clothes, uniform, shoes, etc)

- **$___: Food related**
  (meals out, lunches, snacks, etc)

- **$___: Anything else**

Now add that up for a monthly total, and divide it by the number of hours you work in a given month. To continue our running example, here's some example expenses:

- **$100: Transportation**
  ($100 a month for a public transit pass)

- **$40: Professional appearance**

(**A new $40 blouse every two months; $40/2= $20 a month. New slacks every three months; $60/3=$20 a month**)

- **$32: Food related**
  (**a $4 coffee to go, usually twice a week. $4 times two purchases a week, multiplied by 4 weeks in a month**)

That gives you a total of $172 for the month of expenses directly supporting your employment.

To break that down to what it costs per hour of employment, take the sum of monthly work expenses and divide it by the number of hours you work in a month. In our example it's $172/160 hours (40 hours times 4 weeks = 160 hours). These expenses essentially cost you $1.08 per hour worked. This may not seem like a lot, but it's not to be overlooked. When you compare this to our first example of take home wage, $14.60, subtracting the purchases required to maintain your employment (transportation, clothes, food), your take home drops to $13.52.

Time

We've based all our calculations off of the time you spend working. But rare is the job that all time spent outside those hours is our own. Unless you work from your home, you have a commute. That is time you're required to spend in order to earn your income that's not directly compensated. Estimate the time you spend commuting in a given workday, both to and from work. Divide that by 60 minutes, to get your hourly figure of time spent commuting.

___: Minutes spent commuting each day, roundtrip

÷

60: minutes in an hour

___: hourly figure of time spent commuting

According to the US Census Bureau, the average American commute is 27 minutes, with more than 14 million people now spending an hour or more traveling to work. We'll use this average for our running example:

54: Minutes spent commuting each day, roundtrip

÷

60: minutes in an hour

.9: hourly figure of time spent commuting

Now, we are going to view this time as a "cost" to you—because it is. The time you spend commuting could be considered "part of the job" and therefore a drain on your paycheck. It is an abstract expense but can be viewed in a dollar amount. To assign a dollar amount to the cost of your commute time, you multiply your hourly figure of time spent commuting by your take home wage, with work expenses deducted.

___: hourly figure of time spent commuting

x

$___: Hourly take home wage, work expenses deducted

_____

$___: cost of the time spent commute per day

For our running example:

0.9: hourly figure of time spent commuting

x

$13.52: Hourly take home wage, work expenses deducted

_____

$12.17: cost of the time spent commuting per day

In our example, $12.17 worth of your time isn't compensated. To see how this affects your take home wage, you would first figure how much your take home pay is for a day. In our example, we'd multiply a day's wage, at $13.52, by 8 hours worked. That is $108.16. We then subtract the cost of the time spent commuting round trip per day ($12.17 in the example). That would be $95.99. And to get the hourly wage, we divide that by our hours worked in a day, which is 8 in our example, giving us our new hourly take home pay of $12.00 per hour.

To reiterate, you start out with the baseline thought of "I make $18.58 an hour." But after taxes and deductions, you take home $14.60 hourly in cash. And once you factor in work expenses and commuting time, the things required to actually do your job, it knocks it down to $12.00 an hour.

You could even dig deeper: there's an extremely pervasive culture in America to put in additional time working outside established work hours, especially if you are a salaried worker. There's also time spent interviewing and applying for new jobs. Unpaid labor toward attaining or retaining employment pops up in so many ways.

For these reasons, your hourly wage may feel less impactful than it initially appears.

There are a lot of factors that chip away at that rate you agreed to be paid in income. It's one of the hardest gut punches of personal finance: you can almost certainly think you have more money coming in than you actually do. We started with the example of $18.58/hr before taxes, but it dwindled down to $12/hr after making concessions for costs for maintaining your employment and time spent commuting. That's a 35% difference. Speaking in gross hourly incomes and salaries before taxes has an inflated effect on the money we think we have available to us.

You may think your take home wage is measly. And maybe it is, but it's your starting point. You know where you stand, and while it's a small consolation prize, this is a big step in making fiances less scary: thoroughly and honestly knowing your situation.

YOUR RECEIPT
THANK YOU
11/09/2020   10:20m
0000 #9673

ITEM $30.00

IX $3.08

CASH $33.08

4

SPENDING MONEY

Y ou might be thinking "oh I *know* how to spend money 😋 💰 💸" And you're right— if you've made a dollar in this life, you know how purchasing things works; you go to the convenience store, you see a soda pop you're craving, you give the clerk your money, and you get to take that sweet beverage and be on your way.

What I'm talking about is the grand collective idea of spending money. About all the things you've been buying recently, all the debts that you are currently paying off, and all the things you'd like to buy in the future.

We're going to compare the amount you currently spend in a month to the amount you currently make in a month. The good news is, we already have part of the calculating work done. We know exactly how much you make; it's your effective hourly wage from the previous chapter. For simplicity's sake, let's start with the initial simple hourly "take home" wage: your net income, divided by the hours worked for that net income.

In this chapter we're going to look at spending in monthly chunks, so we'll need to calculate your effective monthly wage: take home hourly wage multiplied by the hours worked in a given month (160 for full-time, but count your hours if you work part time or have multiple jobs) = monthly "take home" income. Fill in yours below:

$___: hourly "take home" wage

x

___: The hours worked in a month

$___ Monthly "take home" income

To carry over our median American in Chicago example from last chapter:

$14.60: hourly "take home" wage

x

160: The hours worked in a month
(40 hours a week, multiplied by 4 weeks in a month = 160)

$2336 Monthly "take home" income

Again, please don't be discouraged if your amount is less than the example; 50% of people are making less than that example.

Tracking your spending for one month

Alright, so we know how much you make, but to get a full financial picture, we need to track how much you spend. For the sake of this exercise, I'd recommend tracking your spending for at least a month. I know it seems like a long time, but we'll be using this spending log as a resource throughout this chapter, so keep it handy!

There are two main strategies to track your spending; the easy way, and the hard way:

Easy

If you mostly/always use a credit and/or debit card, you can pull up your monthly statements (often online, but they may also mail them to you monthly) and see all the transactions you've made in a given month.

Hard

If you use mostly cash, or even a mix of cash and credit/debit, I'd recommend starting some sort of log to list out all your transactions for that month. I've included a template below, but you could also use a list on your phone, a notebook, a spreadsheet—whatever you think you'll be able to faithfully and diligently do. There are even free websites and apps that can help you with this task.

This is all about getting the most complete picture you can, so even if you go the "easy" route, there are additional things to consider:

- **Random transactions:** Record transactions in cash, check, Venmo, PayPal, and any other slippery ways cash gets away from us that won't appear on your bank statement.

- **Annual expenses:** Create a list of things that you pay for in a lump sum, such as yearly memberships, magazine subscriptions, renters insurance, annual pet vet visits, etc. Divide that amount by 12 to consider it as part of your monthly spend, even if you already paid for it this year, or have yet to pay for it. It helps with that dreaded "something always comes up" feeling if you've tried budgeting before.

And as a conciliatory note: tracking your spending is not fun. It can be really uncomfortable. But think of it as a skill you are developing. It might feel awkward, even depressing at first, but be gentle with yourself; you'll find your rhythm with it.

Date	Item/Service Purchased	Amount Spent

Annual Expense	Amount Spent	Amount Spent divided by 12

Total: $ _____

After your month of tracking your spending, add together all your purchases from the month for a grand total. Don't forget to include any yearly purchases, divided to a monthly rate. Write in that sum total here:

$_____

Total Monthly Spending

This can be a real gut-punch moment. No matter how large or small the figure you wrote above is, it's really, really hard to reconcile your spending into a single lump sum.

Do you spend less than you make?

Now that we've done the math, we're at a moment of truth. We're going to compare your monthly take home to your monthly spending.

Which amount is larger?	
Monthly take home income	Total monthly spending
Congrats, you are ending the month with more in your pocket than you started. But I won't tell you that you can skip the rest of the book; this is just the first signpost on our path to financial wellness. You're starting off on the right foot, but there's more to learn ahead.	This is a problem. Because you're spending more than you make, you are at best just scraping by, and at worst, digging yourself into debt. We'll need to see what adjustments can be made, but you're on the right track just doing this exercise.

Needs before wants

It seems black and white, but it's actually almost all grays. There's a lot more nuance to this topic than "needs = good spending; wants = bad spending."

We, as modern people, desire a whole gamut of things. We want to be safe, entertained, and respected. You can buy a whole lot of things to get you to that end. But I'm sure you haven't forgotten the burn of the previous exercise; coming up with a concrete number of how much money you typically spend, contrasted with the amount of cash you have coming in. There are limits to the lifestyle you can afford, and in this you should prioritize the things that help you survive (and also live comfortably).

In economics, needs and wants can be seen as two ends of a spectrum—a "need" is defined as something needed to literally survive, traditionally defined as food, water, and shelter. A "want" is something that a person desires to have, but does not need in order to survive. It's a tad unrealistic to approach your budget with these two rigid categories. There are things that we could live without, and while there are financial advantages of being super frugal, there are trade-offs. You could not have a car, but you then depend on public transit. You need food, but going to a restaurant might be considered a want. You may have started a family and now need a bigger apartment. All these examples are just to say there is a vast grey area between a need and a want and it is different from person to person, situation to situation.

To see what you personally define as "needs" and "wants" I'm going to challenge you to a variant of the highlighter test created by Manisha Thakor, a financial advisor, author, and founder of Money Zen. First, grab your spending log, and two highlighters of different colors. If your spending log is digital, decide on a highlighting system. Look at each item on your list of purchases, and using a highlighter, color the rows by this system:

- **Color A:** expenses that are essential to your survival and are imperative to your quality of life.

- **Color B:** expenses that aren't necessarily essential but you are so happy you purchased, you smile at the thought of it and think "no regrets, totally worth it."

Anything in Color A is obviously a need. Items in Color B are wants that have given you a lot of enjoyment. Items that aren't highlighted could also be safely considered a want, and because they aren't inspiring a ton of love, they could potentially be avoided in future purchasing.

Spending Summary

With this freshly highlighted spending log, let's sort the individual purchases you've made into groups. If there are purchases like a morning coffee you make many times throughout the month, add them together. You could group together all your expenses related to your health as one big category, or break it into smaller groups, like prescriptions, therapy, and gym membership. I've added some major categories to get you started, but feel free to cross them out if they don't apply. There's lots of blanks so be as specific to you as you like, but I included a general list of categories as well if you get stuck.

Needs		Wants	
Rent/mortgage payment	$____	Clothing	$____
Renters/homeowners insurance	$____	Books	$____
Utilities: gas, electric	$____	Morning coffee	$____
Groceries	$____	Zine printing	$____
	$____		$____
	$____		$____
	$____		$____
	$____		$____
	$____		$____
	$____		$____
	$____		$____
	$____		$____
TOTAL:	$____		$____

HOME: Internet, laundry, furniture, cleaning supplies

HEALTH: Doc appts, Rx, dentist, ad hoc medical/dental, over the counter drugs

PETS: Food, vet, grooming, toys, treats

DEBT: Student loan debt payment, credit card debt payment, medical debt payment, car payment

SOCIAL: Gifts (birthdays, holidays), date nights, outings with friends, postage

TECH: Cell phone, digital subscriptions (Netflix, Hulu, Prime, SquareSpace), computer payment plan, software

PERSONAL: Hobbies, snacks, coffee, gym membership, haircuts, art supplies, make up, Christmas cards, photobooths

TRAVEL: Air fare, train tickets, public transit, accommodations (hotels, hostels, etc), Uber, bike rental, gasoline (tip: if you take a few tips a year, try to divide it out to a monthly cost)

ENTERTAINMENT: Concerts, video games, movies, alcohol/weed, restaurants, fast food, board games, magazine subscriptions

Balancing Your Budget with 50/20/30

The work of recording, reviewing, and sorting your expenses is tedious to say the least. Further still, it can seem difficult to put all these numbers into meaningful context.

Let's zoom out from the trees to see the forest; let's use a tool to create an overview and check the overall balance of your income and spending to be sure that you're saving, and to allow you to enjoy the more frivolous things you choose to indulge in without guilt. Coined by Senator Elizabeth Warren, it's a simple ratio: 50% of your income on needs, 20% towards savings, and 30% for your "wants."

Conjure that "monthly take home income" figure from page 58. Let's divide that along this ratio:

50% "effective monthly income" = $____ in needs per month

20% "effective monthly income" = $____ in savings per month

30% "effective monthly income" = $____ in wants per month

So in our running example, with the $2336 effective monthly income:

50% = $1168 in needs per month

20% = $467 in savings per month

30% = $701 in wants per month

Flip back to page 66, your spending summary, and plug in the sum total each of your Needs and Wants columns.

$___: Current spending on needs

$___: Current spending on wants

Finally, we'll see how much you're saving each month. Add together current spending on needs and current spending on wants and subtract that from your monthly take home income. Ideally, this number is positive, but if you're spending more than you make, it will be negative. Either way, write it in below.

$___: Current monthly savings

No matter how good or bad your situation, the fact is that you now have a fully realized outlook on where you are at financially. Plus, we're basically done with all the intensely personal math!

You can now clearly and honestly see the balance of what you're spending on needs and wants, and how much you're saving. If your ratios are close to 50/20/30, that's great, and if they're a bit off, you can identify with ease where the rebalances need to happen.

All the exercises you've completed thus far have been surveying where you're currently at. Now we're going to talk about where to go next.

Tailoring and Maintaining the Budget

So where do we start with changes? Well, the 50/20/30 budget is a great thing to aspire to, but it's not the one and only, pass fail, gold standard; the ratios can easily be tailored to your situation. It's all about having an intentional, realistic balance, while making room for savings in it all.

For instance, if you live in an area with a high cost of living, such as New York or San Francisco, it's probably not feasible to have all your needs be covered by just 50% of your income. Maybe having 70% of your income go towards needs, 20% on wants, and 10% towards savings is a more sustainable ratio for you.

Another example is if you're aggressively paying down debt, maybe it's helpful for you to divide the "savings" aspect of the ratio into its own additional component. You could see it as 50% needs, 10% debt repayment, 10% savings, 30% wants.

And of course life is full of unexpected plot twists; injuries, job loss, pandemics. If your expenses balloon or your income disappears, you'll inherently have to reconsider your spending.

But, when things are stable, aiming for a variant of the 50/20/30 budget will keep you housed, fed, entertained, and preparing for a rainy day—which is exactly what a good budget should do.

However, you might find yourself in an unsustainable imbalance, in which case, you'll need to reconsider and adjust where your money goes. Look at your current ratio of spending on needs, savings, and wants, and make smaller goals to reach your ideal ratio, be it 50/20/30 or otherwise. To do this, you'll need to keep on tracking your expenses. Set a small attainable ratio goal, and check in at the end of the month by adding up your needs, wants, and savings. Kind of a drag, but with time it will feel great to see your improvements.

For example, maybe you're currently at 60% needs, 0% savings, and 40% wants. Maybe you trim a few want purchases, reconsider some of those needs, and/or explore options for more income.

After a month or two you've managed to negotiate some "need" expenses down and increased your income by taking on a few more hours at work, and your ratios are closer to 55% needs, 10% savings, and 35% wants.

Maybe you start to cut back on some of those want-to-have purchases to bulk up your savings, and you ask for a raise after working those extra hours. After a couple more months, you're close to 55% needs, 15% savings, and 30% wants. And so on.

Notice that these changes took months to make. It may seem like the easiest way to shift the balance is to cut all "nonessentials" out from your purchasing. Like a fad diet, it probably won't stick; you'll get frustrated with the deprivation and give up. It's important to consider all the ways you can shift your budget, from increasing income, to negotiating down the cost of needs, and yes, reevaluating your more frivolous purchases. This is about attainable, consistent improvement, not immediate results.

Tips on Curbing Expenses

It wouldn't be a personal finance book if it didn't have a section on ways to curb spending!

I'm half joking (there are some actual tips coming, I promise), but there is a certain sense of dread I feel when I think about ways to further eliminate my own spending, or offer these tips to others. I do feel like I need to put a little disclaimer/human empathy/greater system note in here that I touched on earlier:

We are living in an era where my generation (Millennials) are widely predicted to become the first generation in U.S. history to do worse than their parents financially, not due to lack of trying, but a surge in financial inequality. The cost of college and healthcare skyrocketed in the past two decades, as purchasing power has failed to rise, and home ownership isn't as good of a source of equity as it used to be. Rugged, you're-on-your-own individualism is what is supposed to guarantee us success, but 78 percent of U.S. workers live paycheck to paycheck to make ends meet. According to *The Nation*, the top 1 percent of Americans now take home, on average, more than 40 times the incomes of the bottom 90 percent. They capitalized on devalued assets during the 2008 meltdown, and continue to amass greater and greater wealth in the recovery. There are larger economic forces at play that affect your living experience more than if you pack your lunch every day, and they are impossible for a single person to change.

deep sigh

There are lots and lots of tips out there of how to trim a few dollars here and there from your spending. And they can be super helpful! But they are so plentiful elsewhere, and I'm going to give you the benefit of the doubt; you probably know a lot of them already. Pack your lunch, skip the morning coffee, cancel subscriptions you don't use. These are all great ideas (I do them myself) but I'd rather focus on some larger changes and more fundamental challenges to a typical consumer mindset.

This quote is so nice I'm using it twice: **"Spend extravagantly on the things you love, and cut costs mercilessly on the things you don't."** —Ramit Sethi, personal finance writer. It's great advice: give your money and attention to things that give you the most joy, and deliberately spend as little as possible on the things that aren't important to you. Warren Buffett, legendary investor, has a variation on this as well: the **5/25 rule**. First, you list out 25 things you'd like to accomplish, no limits. You then do the difficult task of ranking them in order of priority. Spoiler: the top 5 are the ones to focus on and the other 20 are what Buffett calls "Avoid-At-All-Cost list." He posits that "no matter what, these things get no attention from you until you've succeeded with your top 5." Whether you agree or not, the thrust is still the same: decide what the most important things are to you, and be selective. You already have a highlighted list of things you're happy to have spent money on (you're welcome!). Use that as a starting point to see what you truly love, and what you passively like.

On a similar note: *Just stop worrying about what other people think, as well as what other people spend money on.* What a person spends their money on (or decides not to spend money on) is their business and theirs alone. Personal finance is, well, personal. A lot of my advice on curbing purchases is going to be self-reflective and, ideally, have the side benefit of not only putting your money towards things that you actively love and support (or contribute to your survival) but also towards your own sense of contentment.

If you struggle with impulse purchases, there's a lot of power to be had in a **"Should I Buy This?"** question. It's basically a simple, specific question you ask yourself before making a purchase that wasn't planned. There are lots of variations of this, so it's important to select or write your own question that really resonates with you:

- Can I really afford it?

- What will I do with it?

- Could I borrow it from someone?

- How often will I use it?

- Could I ask my social network about borrowing it?

- Could I get it second hand?

- Could I make it myself?

- Can I delay it?

- Is there a lower-cost solution?

- Have I searched online for a discount?

Or one I use personally:

- What does this item do for me that nothing else does?

A companion to the "should I buy this question" is giving yourself time to think on a purchase. In our era of infinitely available commodities, it's rare there is a purchase you could make today that wouldn't be available tomorrow. J.D. Roth from the blog Get Rich Slowly called it his **30-day rule.** Basically, if you're interested in buying something that's a bit of a whim, put it down, and write it on a list with the date and price. Give yourself 30 days (or however long you find works for you, even a few days can be a good waiting period) and revisit. You may be surprised how often you're grateful to not have spent the money.

You probably are aware of the benefits of meal planning and sticking to a grocery list. These practices encapsulate several **great habits**:

- Delaying gratification

- Cutting out temptations

- Planning ahead

- Eradicating guilt

A small thing, but consider **eliminating expensive destructive vices.** I'm sure you could make an argument that if these things brought you joy or relief, then why not. I'm not here to make a moral stance, but from a purely financial perspective, these simply aren't the best investments of your money.

- Never play the lottery: the odds are so incredibly not in your favor. Your money will go farther doing just about anything else than buying a lottery ticket.

- Gambling: again, you probably aren't a professional gambler. If you enjoy the game, go ahead and play online for free, or set up a card night with friends. Casinos are built to swindle you.

- Smoking (but also potentially alcohol, soda, coffee and other addictive substances): if you find it difficult to function without any of these, congrats, you are addicted to a substance that may be causing harm to your health, in addition to costing you money. Consider ways to cut back or potentially quit. Keep track of your progress.

And I wanted to end this Spending Money chapter on a very specific note. It's not going to be a surprise to anyone:

Money can't buy happiness (at a certain point)

In 2010, Princeton University conducted a study on the intersection of happiness and income, which gave us the somewhat sensationalized "price of happiness" at making $75,000 a year. People below that rate reported diminishing happiness, and those above it didn't report any higher degree of happiness. There are many interesting aspects of this study, but it seemed to be the catalyst in a subsequent decade of polls, studies, blogs, and books about how money actually can buy happiness. You've probably heard the advice to spend your money on experiences, not things; that experiences will net more happiness. The KonMari method of curating your entire life with only belongings that "spark joy" (and disposing of the rest) also was popularized in this time. There's additional studies that have found that there are two purely financial pursuits resulting in solid improvements in well being: getting out of debt and donating to charity.

I'm not saying any of these claims aren't true, but they can be overly generalized. One of the most unexpected benefits I gained on my personal finance journey is the self reflection it required of me: What is it that brings me joy? What are my top priorities in this life?

In my personal experience, the purchases that have brought me the most joy have an interpersonal aspect, like coffee dates with friends and sending birthday cards. I have absolutely tried to reduce my fondness of physical possessions, but I've found in actuality there absolutely are "things" bring me a lot of joy, such as quality tools that I use frequently: a quality frying pan, a nice pair of leather shoes, a vintage Caboodle for my makeup. And there's also the knick knacks that I've collected over the years; while some people may see that as clutter, I treasure them. But I also have a controversial methodology when it comes to book ownership—primarily loaned from the library or a friend and very selectively purchased. I'm not trying to convince anyone to stop buying books; rather, this is a value I've cultivated for myself.

There are endless things to spend your money on, and some of them will bring you more happiness than others.

But I am of the mind that the only way money can truly bring you a lasting sense of happiness is by reducing your stress and eventually improving your life options through improved financial security.

5

SAVING MONEY

Like helmets, seatbelts, and insurance, building up your savings account is meant to protect you. It also can feel like a real slog. But there is a sexy side to savings: trips to glamorous locations, finally adopting a pet, buying a home of your own. That's right, setting savings goals can help you acquire the finer things in life.

I'm sure you know saving is important, but beyond knowing that it's the responsible thing to do, why save?

Having well funded savings accounts gives you peace of mind. Should some unexpected expense come up, it helps prevent chaos from ensuing. You have time and choices available instead of immediately stressing out and resorting to expensive loans or credit cards. Over time, you can actually work towards more enticing goals like travel or a new bike. In the long term, saving will help you be able to retire from working while maintaining a comfortable lifestyle.

You may think just having a savings account you throw $50 into every once in a while is enough. It's a great start, but there is a strategy around how to structure and consider your savings.

Emergency F*ck off Fund

We have to start with the goal that is, on its face, pretty terrible: saving for unforeseen tragedy. It has a common name that isn't very inspiring (emergency fund), so the alternative I'll present to you is what writer Paulette Perhach dubbed it on the personal finance blog The Billfold: The F*ck Off Fund.

This is a dedicated stash of cash set aside for the unexpected, the urgent, and the costly. Specific instances you may want to have a tidy sum tucked away for are:

- Job loss

- Medical emergency

- Unplanned travel, such as for a family emergency

- Unexpected repairs on a home or vehicle

- Or the titular need to tell someone to F*ck off: being able to confidently leave a terrible employer or terrible living situation

To begin your own emergency fund, you simply need to open a savings account dedicated solely to this purpose. The funds in this account should be considered off limits, except for, well, emergencies, like those listed above. The advice on exactly how much you should save in an emergency fund ranges, but a good goal is 3 months living expenses (the total of "needs" and "wants" which we calculated in chapter 5). Fill in your amount below:

$____: 3 Months of living expenses

I'm sure that number feels big, but some personal finance writers even suggest 6 months (or more!). The important thing isn't necessarily the exact size of the account, but just having some dedicated funds for emergencies only, and building up towards that 3 month goal. If you're just starting your emergency fund, start small. Find an amount that you can put aside each pay period, and try to build up to a single month's worth of expenses. You may need to sideline some of your "want" expenses until you get that first month saved. It's not fun. It's probably the least fun thing, deciding to not buy fun things in order to save for the inevitability of terrible things happening. But hopefully it can give you a sense of security; it's the net beneath the tightrope.

Once you have a month of living expenses in your emergency fund, do a dance, sing a song, hug a friend. It's a huge accomplishment that, while it can feel like you have nothing to show for, is the first step towards a financially secure standing. If something unforeseeable happens, you can weather the storm! If you have an intolerable situation, you have some flexibility to leave it!

Free money and 401(k)s

Once you've got at least a month's worth of savings in your f*ck off fund, see if your current employer offers you free money. That may sound like pure fantasy, what kind of company just gives away free money? Lots of them do! It's just usually through a retirement savings investment account called a 401(k). That all may sound drab at first, but it's still potentially free money.

As a very general concept, you can think of a 401(k) as a special kind of savings account that an employer deposits free money in for you to use when you retire. At its core, the goal of a 401(k) is to incentivize individuals to sock away money for retirement, and to be an attractive perk a company can offer employees.

More specifically, 401(k)s are tax-advantaged investment accounts. Employers typically contribute a set percentage of an employee's salary, and employees have the option of contributing to it from their own wages. The fund grows tax free for decades, and you pay the tax when you withdraw funds in retirement. The money in these accounts is invested in mutual funds made up of a mix of stocks, bonds, and money market investments.

The kicker of the free money is that it's meant to be utilized in retirement, not immediately. If you withdraw before you're 59.5 years old, there are fees and taxes on withdrawals (with a few exceptions, like buying a first home). Also, while investments typically grow over long periods of time, they are investing in the market; financial gains are expected but not guaranteed.

There are a few other variables company to company. First off, not every job offers a 401(k) program. If they do offer it, employers may require you to work at the company for a set number of months before you can even enroll. While some companies make contributions to their employee's 401(k)s with no strings attached, some require a "match", meaning that for every percentage of your salary you contribute to your 401(k), they'll make a contribution to match (you put in 3% of your salary, they deposit that amount additionally). Ask your manager or HR representative if they have a 401(k) program, what the company contributes, and if/when you're eligible.

Despite all the jargon, 401(k)s are kind of a set and forget it thing: after deciding on contributions, the most you'll do is decide what fund you'd like to have the account invested in. Some employers manage this choice for you. If you leave the company, you get to keep your 401(k); however, you shouldn't withdraw the funds directly. To avoid fees and taxes, it's a smarter move to roll the account over into your next employer's 401(k).

401(k)s may seem really intimidating, and honestly some of the paperwork can be daunting. But if your employer makes contributions on your behalf, the best thing you can do is just open the account.

If you are able to cnroll in a 401(k) plan, and your company makes a contribution without a match, great! That truly is just free money towards your retirement. If they do require that you make a contribution yourself that they then match, I really encourage you to opt in; not only are you saving for your future but you're also getting that free money. It may sting to take home slightly less money, especially when you've already been diligently saving, but... It's free money!!! And I promise you will not regret it when you hit retirement; that money will likely be worth much more than the initial deposits after years of compounding interest (more on that in chapter 9).

Also, if you just skimmed that section because you're self employed or your employer does not offer a 401(k), that's okay! It's still worth knowing how 401(k)s work in case a future employer does offer it.

A note on debt

Before we go further on our saving journey, I have to ask: do you have any debt? Student loans, medical bills, credit cards, etc? Not all debt is the same. Some kinds of debts are much more expensive to carry than others. The way to know which debt is your most diabolical is knowing the interest rate: the percentage fee that you're paying on top of the debt you owe. If you have any debts with interest rates higher than 10%, I recommend redirecting your efforts from saving goals to debt repayment. Head over to chapter 6 for more on that.

But let's say you don't have any high interest debt, which is great! From here, most personal finance gurus would advise you to keep growing your emergency fund from 1 month's worth of expenses to 3 months, if not more. And I absolutely think that is a great idea, that is actually what I too would advise, you should 100% totally do that. However, I can also imagine that if you are at the stage of having just built up your savings and knocking back your high debts, you may be feeling a little demotivated about saving even more money for bad stuff happening to future you. You've come really far, and I want you to begin to see the magic and positivity of savings, beyond just being secure if tragedy strikes (even though that's super important!). Because you can, and should, practice saving for something nice you actually want, such as an item of clothing or a trip, by making a plan and achieving it.

Savings goals

Creating a savings goal has simple steps: pick something you want that's meaningful to you, research how much it costs, be realistic, and know how long it will take.

No matter where you're at in your savings journey, it's important to have a purpose in mind. The purpose of an emergency fund is to have financial security for the unknown future. But you could have a savings goal for any number of things: a new computer, a trip with your best friend, or buying a friggin' house! And the meaning behind something you want is important to consider as well: why do you want the new computer? Maybe you work from home and it would improve your enjoyment and efficiency on the job. Maybe you are an avid gamer and you're looking to upgrade your machine with the best display. It doesn't matter what the reason is, so long as it is a reason that personally motivates you. That's the key: the motivation. Because saving, by its very nature, as I'm sure you appreciate by now, means having to opt out of other purchases or increase your income somehow. Having a purpose to your savings is a powerful motivator towards saving for that end goal.

The second part of a savings goal is the actual tactical part: the cost, the time, and the reality. It's really fun to daydream about far flung vacations, but it's also easy to say "I'd love to go to Paris, but I could never afford it." And maybe that's true, but what if it's not? We live in the age of the internet search; you can research and create an educated estimate as to the cost of a trip without that much difficulty. For the humble savings goal, you don't need an exact figure to start; an informed ballpark estimate will do.

For instance, the trip to Paris. Literally just searching "how much does a trip to Paris cost for a week" gave me a website that already did the breakdown and came to $2,150. Perfect, that's a great starting point! That may seem like a lot, but you're not trying to go to Paris tomorrow, are you? What's a good figure you think you could save a month? Let's say, $50 a month. That would put your trip out 43 months, or 3.5 years. Trying to go sooner than that? Could you swing $90 a month? That's just two years!

So let's just try it out. This doesn't have to be *the* savings goal, but just as an exercise:

- What is something you'd like to do or have?

- How much does it cost? Do some research if you aren't sure.

- How soon would you want to reach this savings goal? Divide the cost by the number of months.

- Or if you already have a set amount of money you want to set aside each month for the goal, divide the total cost by the monthly savings, and you'll get the number of months until you reach the goal.

And something magical happens when you start a savings goal; as you watch the savings grow, you feel proud that you've managed it, and it makes the anticipation of the goal all the sweeter. And something even more magical happens: over time, these feelings may inspire you to put a little bit more aside each month. Maybe you do a freelance job you weren't expecting, or you get a little extra cash during the holidays. These may be good little windfalls to put towards your goal.

The great thing about a savings goal is that it can be small, it can be big, but as long as it's meaningful and the cost and time are realistic for your situation, you can actually get the things you want! For me, I love giving gifts during the holidays, but I hated feeling like I was overspending those last weeks of December. So I set a savings goal for gifts that I put $40 a month in all year. I have had goals for getting a dog ($2,000) and going on trips (Japan $4,000, Aruba $1,000, Madison, WI $100). Some took months, some took years. Having a purpose and a plan can go a long way towards keeping spending temptations at bay, with a bonus of putting those savings towards something really important to you.

Advanced savings strategies

Just a quick note before we end this chapter on savings: if it feels like there's more to say on the topic, it's because there is. If you want to radically build up your savings, or have a lot of goals, and/or lots of debt, there are totally strategies to manage it, but my conceit of this book isn't for those fine-tune bits. Trust me, if you prioritize a fully funded emergency savings account and carry no debt, or even just low-interest debt (less than 4%), you are doing amazing!

6

OWING MONEY

Being in debt is no fun. Making payment on debts can feel like you're throwing your money into a deep endless void, watching it get sucked into a black hole. It's so not fun, many people disassociate from their debt, throwing away notices and finding any number of ways to push it out of their minds. But you've probably realized the through line here of how we're dealing with these big ugly topics: we're going to look at this mess, break it down to its basic components, and get ourselves on track towards a better situation.

What is debt?

Debt is when you purchase something, but instead of paying for it fully at the time, you pay later, generally at an agreed upon rate, over a given period of time. Fundamentally, if you are spending more than you earn, you are heading towards being in debt. However, you can also become in debt when you seek out a loan for a large purchase (a car, a home, college, etc.) Being in debt entails owing money to a lender (such as a bank, a credit card company, a student loan provider, or maybe even a friend) that you pay off in payments, typically along with a fee called interest (APR, annual percentage rate). Interest is usually written as a percentage fee that's added to your monthly payment. Generally (and currently, these are subject to change with a given economy), a low interest rate would be something around 2-4%; mortgages typically can have a rate in this range. A high interest rate would be around 16%, which is the average credit card interest rate as of this writing. These rates can vary depending upon your credit history (more on that later).

Always being debt free is a great goal, but sometimes it's not the smartest financial choice. Saving up until you can pay a full college tuition probably isn't as wise as going sooner and taking out student loans. It could take a long time to save enough, tuition rates are rising each year, and you might get a higher salary with a college degree. In a few categories, going into debt is nearly unavoidable, such as mortgages and medical debt.

It is really simple to say "don't get into debt" but the reality of the situation is many of us live on a knife's edge. 78% of American workers are living paycheck to paycheck. This means roughly one in four people don't (or simply can't) set aside any savings each month, exposing themselves to risk. Without savings, a single emergency can put them in debt, either by the cost of the event itself or worse, the emergency means they aren't able to work, putting them in a debt spiral. (Another depressing plug for the importance of an emergency fund). And this situation is kind of the norm. 71% of all workers say they are in debt, and while 46% feel their debt is manageable, 56% say they feel they will be in debt for their entire life.

And it bears saying—all debt comes with consequences beyond just your financial standing. Whether it's a health emergency, a mortgage, or a spending spree, it affects your emotional and psychological wellbeing. Being in debt has been clinically proven to be linked with higher rates of stress, anxiety, and depression. Other dismal effects arise like constantly worrying about money, experiencing intense feelings of being overwhelmed with no end in sight, and resentment towards a partner, a boss, or even yourself. There are so many negative emotions that are strongly tied to debt: anger, frustration, regret, shame, embarrassment, fear. If you're in debt, these feelings are totally valid; however, don't let them stop you from bettering your situation. As The Simple Dollar founder Trent Hamm has said, "Debt freedom isn't just freedom from debt. It's freedom from worry." Your wellbeing is invaluable, and sometimes it's hard won.

Put it on plastic: Credit cards

A credit card is a financial product in which you are given a card similar to a debit card, but it operates with a key difference: when you swipe it, it doesn't immediately take the money from your checking account. Instead, the credit card company pays the vendor on your behalf. At the end of the month, you receive a bill from the credit card company for the sum total of all the purchases you made with the credit card that month. If you aren't able to pay the entire balance, they allow you to pay a portion of what is owed, but they tack on an interest fee which can get pretty hefty. If you continue to pay less than the full amount owed, the balance keeps increasing, along with their interest fees. This is how people sink into credit card debt. However, if you follow this rule, you will never, ever get into credit card debt: *pay it off, in full, on time, every month.*

In the best of times, you wouldn't purchase anything on a credit card you couldn't afford in cash, but many people have credit cards "for emergencies." Ideally you have an emergency fund, so if unexpected expenses come up, you have cash to cover it. But if you don't have enough cash on hand and need a short term loan, a credit card can give you at least a few weeks before the bill is due to drum up some extra funds. Carrying a balance is a slippery slope into debt, so you'll want to do your best to pay it off in full as soon as possible.

There are perks to using a credit card: earning "points" to be redeemed for cash, travel, gifts cards, and more. They also tend to offer some consumer protections, like extended warranties and identity theft protection. Another advantage of having a credit card means you build a credit history. When used responsibly, you build a history that proves you are a reliable consumer, which can pay off in instances when your credit report might be pulled: applying for a home loan is a big one, but even an employer or landlord can ask to check your credit history (more on that to come). The big catch to a credit card is the interest rate, that fee you're charged for carrying debt. But, if you pay your credit card balance off, in full, on time, every month, you'll never be charged the interest fee.

Best case scenario with a credit card:

Let's say you applied for a credit card account that has an $8,000 limit and 14.7% interest rate. You chose it based on the rewards program, earning a point per dollar spent to be redeemed for cash. You are approved and receive the card in the mail, and you use it to buy just about anything you need/have budgeted for: groceries, gas, Netflix, whatever. You get a flat tire that costs $155, but you have your emergency fund, so you're fine with putting it on the card, knowing you have the money to cover it. At the end of the billing cycle (generally a month) you receive the bill (by mail or online) and you see the total is $947.74, and due in 3 weeks. You aren't stressed by that total number because it's within your 50/30/20 budget. Like every month, you pay it off completely (the entire $947.74 this month) from your checking account, before the due date.

(You may even have set up an automatic payment so you never ever miss a payment!). Over time, you build up a good history of being able to use a credit card responsibly, and this pays off when you are negotiating a lower interest rate for a mortgage, saving you thousands of dollars over time!

Amazing, right?

But you're probably more aware of...

The worst case scenario with a credit card:

You applied for a credit card account that has an $8,000 limit and 14.7% interest rate. You are approved and receive the card in the mail, and you use it to buy things you may not be able to afford right now, but you figure you can just pay the minimum on the card and pay it off when you have more money. You get a flat tire that costs $155, and you don't have an emergency fund, so you have to put it on the card. You can't even bring yourself to check the credit card balance. At the end of the billing cycle you receive the bill and you see the total is $1,958.38, and due in 3 weeks. You are stressed by that total number because there's no way you have the money to pay it in full. It's kind of scary, so you try and put it out of your mind. You put it so far out of your mind, you forget to pay the bill until the day after it was due, when you receive a notification that you've been charged a $35 fee for being late with the payment. You are feeling frantic and overwhelmed by the balance, and now the fee, so you decide to just pay the minimum amount the credit card company allows, displayed on your bill, which is $25. You figure this is fine for now and you'll just do way better next month, and cut back on a few things. While you shut this out of your mind, the credit card company now has a balance on your account of $1,968.38 (the original balance, plus the late fee, minus your minimum payment). While you go about your life, the credit card company tacks on the interest you accrue on your debt, a daily percentage (your annual percentage rate, the interest rate, ex:14.7%, divided by 365) which may seem small, but it adds up to $24 over the month, in addition to the other purchases you made. Each month you add more to your debt, and this lowers your credit score. You get to a point where you owe more money on the interest than on what you actually used to purchase things.

Sounds really stressful, right? It's tragically common: 43% of credit card holders carry a balance, with the average being $6,354. But the biggest differences between these two stories is having an emergency fund and using the credit card responsibility.

However, to be completely honest, if you don't think you could resist the temptation to "buy now, pay later" maybe a credit card isn't the right thing for you right now. And that's totally fine! According to Gallup, 29% of Americans don't have a credit card account. Having a credit card does take a degree of knowledge and responsibility to use, and I don't want you to open yourself to problematic habits that will cost you money. But there are benefits to having a credit card, and I'm not talking about points. One of the best benefits of responsibility using a credit card over time seems admittedly boring: growing a high credit score.

Credit Score

As I said earlier, it's a measure of how responsible you've shown to be according to a scoring company, a common one being FICO. They monitor certain aspects of your financial life and calculate a score that lenders evaluate you on, and they offer you higher or lower interest rates based on those scores. If you want to buy a house or car, having a good credit score can save you tens of thousands of dollars over time.

The exact calculations of this score are a "trade secret" but are generally known to be:

35% Payment History

Do you pay consistently, on time?

30% Amounts Owed

Generally, the sweet spot is to only use up to 30% of the credit available to you, so if you have a credit card with a $10,000 limit, then you should try to only use a maximum of $3,000.

15% Length of Credit History

How long have you had the accounts for? Longer tends to equate to more trustworthy in their eyes.

10% Credit Mix

The variety of credit cards, installment loans, etc you have.

10% New Credit

Generally if you've been opening more accounts in a short amount of time, it dings your score.

FICO also represents their scores on a super confusing scale of 300-850, with 300 being the worst and 850 being the best. Percentage breakdown is from Experian, and gives an idea of how the scores are distributed.

300-579	Very Poor	16%
580-669	Fair	17%
670-739	Good	21%
740-799	Very Good	25%
800-850	Exceptional	21%

That may be a lot to soak in. But if you're on the fence about a credit card being right for you, the benefit of opening one to grow your credit score can help you down the road with major purchases.

For example, let's say you want to buy a home, and need a loan for $300,000, and we can see a split screen reality where in one you have an "exceptional" credit score and the other you just have a "fair" credit score.

Exceptional credit score:
The bank offers you an APR of 3.52%

Monthly payment: $1,350

Fair credit score:
the bank offers you an APR of 5.11%

Monthly payment: $1,631

So right off the bat, the difference per month is $281. A pretty sizable difference! But let's stretch this out—a typical home loan is 30 years.

Exceptional credit score:
$1,350 x 12 months x 30 years = $486,000

Fair credit score:

$1,631 x 12 months x 30 years = $587,160

The difference: $101,160!!

So maybe you glossed over that example because you're thinking "I will never buy a home, this doesn't apply to me" that's fine, but like I said before, the benefits of having a good credit score can also affect a landlord or employer's choice to approve your application. Or maybe you have another goal in mind that you'll need a loan for; like a car, or opening a business. In any case, everyone should keep an eye on their credit score and credit report a few times a year:

Check your existing credit score: You can check your score for free on www.creditkarma.com

Review your credit reports: These are different from your score, which is just a single number. This is a detailed report of your credit history (loans taken out, credit cards opened, etc.) and this history is what your credit score is based on. It's important to check these every 4-12 months to check for errors or identity theft. You get three free annual credit reports, one from each of the three credit bureaus. Visit AnnualCreditReport.com to make the request, or call 877-322-8228.

If you'd like strategies on improving your credit score, see chapter 7 on Repairing Money.

Good vs bad (debt)

In addition to credit card debt, there are of course other types of debt: car payments, student loans, mortgages. Sometimes people refer to these as "good debt" and credit card debt being "bad debt." The difference being that good debt is seen as an investment that will gain or generate value overtime, like a college education. Bad debt is the opposite; debt spent on things that quickly lose their value, such as putting a shopping spree on your credit card and holding a balance.

This is where the goal of being debt free takes a personal turn: just like wants and needs, you should decide what debt you're willing to take on for your situation. Buying a house is generally seen as a good investment, but if you can rent for cheaper or plan on moving out of the area within the next decade, it may not be a good idea. A degree is super impactful to your earnings, but with student debt skyrocketing, it can be incredibly costly to ignore the price tag and consider 100K in student debt as "good" debt. All this is to say, just because these types of debt aren't as loathed as credit card debt, they should be approached with great caution and consideration for your situation and goals.

Evil debt

Okay I do think there is some Pure Evil debt out there that you should avoid at all cost: Payday loans or cash advance loans. These places write checks for small loans that you are required to repay, plus interest, when your next paycheck comes (typically two weeks).

The average payday loan in 2016 was $375. The average interest—or "finance charge" as payday lenders refer to it—for a $375 loan would be between $56 at 391% APR and $75 at 521% APR. Many people can't afford to pay it off next payday, and they keep entering into new loans through the same payday lenders, who act like they are helping you. They aren't helping you, they are bleeding you dry, extorting you.[1] 1 in 20 households have taken out a payday loan. It's a 9 billion dollar industry. There are more payday loan businesses than Starbucks or McDonalds. These are predatory loans, which prey on the

---

1 You might be wondering how on Earth this is legal. The Consumer Financial Protection Bureau had written protections during the Obama administration that would require lenders to review someone's financial situation before deeming them eligible for the loan, protecting vulnerable borrowers from getting into these debt cycles. The lending industry lobbied hard against it, and it never went into effect under Trump's administration. In July 2020, they were officially rolled back.

working class and those in impoverished situations who are just scraping by. Payday loans are pure evil. Almost anything you can do to avoid these places is a better deal (see chapter 7 for examples).

Debt Management

So, we've touched on debt as a concept, but the reality of paying it down is a different story.

Again, just a reminder, if you are in any kind of debt, you are not alone; 71% of workers are in debt. It may not be easy, but you can create a plan to get out of debt and work towards financial freedom.

First: get organized

Make a list of all the debts you're carrying and their key details. It's an essential step, but looking at the stone cold numbers can be a really overwhelming experience. Be strong and try to be proud that you're doing this difficult work.

Who is owed	total owed	minimum monthly payment	interest rate	next bill due date	phone #

Decide on some sort of system to keep track of when the payments are due. I recommend a calendar, but a notebook, a spreadsheet, or a series of phone reminders can all work. It just needs to be able to keep track of the day you're going to pay, and how much you're going to pay.

Second: negotiate

Now is the time to see if there's any way to lower the balance you owe and/or the interest rate. Also see if there are any additional assistance or options for paying down the debt. Contacting institutions over the phone tends to work best.

- **Medical and utility debt:** work directly with the hospital, clinic, or utility provider on a repayment plan; ask about any income based discounts if that applies to your situation.

- **Student loans:** income-based repayment plans are available, even deferment may be an option.

- **Mortgage and car loan:** potentially beneficial to refinance if you're in a better financial situation than when you originally applied.

- **Credit card:** ask directly for a lower interest rate or a repayment plan. If they can't help you, you can transfer the balance to a card with an 0% interest intro rate (but make a plan to pay it off before interest kicks back in). If you have more than one credit card debt, it can be good to roll them into one card for simplicity/lower rates, just don't close the empty accounts as that can ding your credit score.

Third: make a plan

You've already worked on your budget, so you should have a good idea of how much money you can dedicate towards the debts. Even if it's not a huge amount, even if it's just the minimum, plan exactly how much you can dedicate towards repayments.

If you only have a single debt, it's clear that you just pay as much as possible on that one debt until it's paid off. But if you have multiple debts, it can be tough to know what to tackle first. There's two approaches to prioritizing, and it definitely depends on your own personality:

- **Snowballing**: after paying the minimum on all your debts, devote any additional available funds to the debt with the smallest balance. Once that debt is cleared, devote the funds you had used each month for the smallest debt towards the next-smallest debt.

- **Avalanche**: very similar to snowball, you pay the minimum on all your debts, and devote any additional available funds to the debt with the highest interest rate. After paying down that debt, you devote those funds towards the debt with the second highest interest rate.

From a numbers standpoint, the avalanche method will technically save you a little more money than the snowballing method. However, a 2012 study from the Kellogg School of Management showed that people with large balances are more likely to stick with their debt payoff plan if they focus on smaller balances first, aka the snowball method. The important thing is to choose a plan and see what motivates you, because that's ultimately what's going to work.

Either way, denote the days on your calendar (or calendar alternative) when your bills are due and the amount you will pay. Pick the debt you'd like to focus on eliminating first and note exactly how much you are going to dedicate towards that debt each month.

Fourth: stick to (or adjust) your plan

A step of its own—sticking to your plan. Do the work of making the payments, keeping your spending in check, and making those big lump payments towards busting each individual debt. Hopefully you start feeling a tiny bit of pride seeing that light at the end of the tunnel. If something about your plan isn't working, adjust it. Maybe you switch from avalanche to snowball, or re-try a negotiating tactic from step two, or a paper calendar instead of one online. And don't forget to celebrate the wins along the way!

Debt should be entered into with caution and care, and paid down as aggressively as possible. Repayment can feel hopeless, but with a plan, you can make your way out of it. Taking steps towards freedom from debt will not only be good for your bottom line, but it will build your financial confidence.

7

REPAIRING MONEY

Thus far, all the advice has been pretty straightforward, but you may be in a less than ideal position already. Maybe you're in a straight-up terrible situation right now. There's nothing left to trim from your spending. The income you have just isn't enough. You may have a poor credit score, or are having a hard time even getting a bank account. It sucks to be in a bind, and sometimes it's not easy to get through. We'll cover some issues you may face in your financial life, how to deal with them, and what resources are out there to help you along the way.

Loss of income

Losing your income is a huge blow to any financial plan, especially when it's unexpected. If you lost your job through no fault of your own, like being laid off, you can apply for unemployment insurance through your state (directory at www.careeronestop.org). Exact eligibility and the rate paid out varies by state as well as your previous income level. Nationally, the average is $473 a week, with a cap of 26 weeks. If you quit your job voluntarily or were fired for misconduct, you won't be eligible for unemployment insurance payments.

After looking into unemployment, it's time to update your budget. If you already completed the 50/20/30 budgeting exercise in chapter 4, revisit your list of spending needs (rent, utilities, groceries, car payments, etc.) and wants (subscriptions, dining out, gym membership, etc.) Decide if there's anything that, given this new context, can be temporarily lowered or eliminated from your spending. Compare the money you have on hand (in checkings, savings, and emergency fund) to how much you anticipate needing to spend monthly. Ideally, you have enough to stay out of debt for at least a month or two.

Start your job search immediately. As soon as you can, update your resume. According to indeed.com, it takes about nine weeks to find a new job. Depending on your industry, the state of the economy, and your personal circumstances; it could take much shorter, or much longer. About one in five of all unemployed people are still looking after 27 weeks. If you're comfortable, tell your community you're looking for work. Create a list of job boards and career pages to check and send out applications regularly. Keep a log of jobs applied, follow up after a few weeks on jobs that you're especially interested in.

After making initial cuts to your spendings and starting your job search, you may have a better idea of how long this period of partial/no income may last. You may need to consider other forms of income: short term jobs such as temp agencies, gig work, baby sitting, walking dogs, or selling possessions like electronics, furniture, or clothes.

If the situation is especially dire (such as high unemployment, in a pandemic, with a tanking economy) you may need to further rethink your situation: where you live (in the city, roommates, moving in with family) and broadening the scope of your job search (part time, contract, a different use of your skillset, or a different field entirely). Community help through mutual aid or crowd funding may also be options. If your employment situation is making you feel hopeless, you might also consider seeking out a career counselor or career therapist. They both can offer guidance in major shifts in job directions, from both tactical and emotional aspects. Openpathcollective.org offers affordable sliding scale services in-office and online. And through all this, be sure to take care of yourself physically and mentally. Know that your value as a human is not tied to your ability to earn income, and this tough situation is temporary.

Getting a checking account when you've made banking mistakes

If you're just scraping by with your checking account, and your balance dips into the negative, your bank may close your account on you. Usually this happens after a set number of days with a negative balance or if they suspect fraud (writing bad checks). Some states require notice be given before they close your account, some states don't. And while they can't discriminate on race or gender, if your account goes delinquent, they are legally allowed to close it.

As soon as you get the notice of your account closing, the quicker you handle it, the better off you'll be. First, stop any direct deposits you have to that closed account. You will not be able to access any funds coming into that closed account, and the bank may keep it to cover any negative balance. Talk to your HR department or manager about changing your payment to a check, or route it to a different bank account if you have one. Then cancel, suspend, or reroute any automatic payments for bills or transfers linked to that account. Once you've done that, you should try to work it out directly with the bank if possible: call or visit to find out exactly why the account was closed, find out the total damage with overdraft charges and fees, and ask to set up a repayment plan in writing.

It's important to work with your bank after they've closed your account, as they've likely already reported it to ChexSystems, which is similar to a credit report agency, but for banking specifically. Because other banks will be able to see your closed account via ChexSystems, they may not want to open an account with you. Being able to provide a written repayment plan can help sway them.

Another option with a less than stellar bank history is applying for a "second chance" checking account. There are a few drawbacks to these accounts: usually a monthly fee, potentially requiring a direct deposit, or a money management class. But, if you demonstrate that you can manage the second chance account well, many institutions will allow you to upgrade to a standard checking account in 6-12 months, given that you demonstrate proper account use. A few banks offer second chance accounts nationwide: Green Dot Bank, Radius Bank, and Wells Fargo. If you're looking for something local, seek out credit unions or community banks, as opposed to major banks that rarely offer these accounts.

If you don't want to go the second chance route, an alternative would be a prepaid debit card. This is a debit card that doesn't have a bank account attached; you simply pre-load it with money. They don't improve your banking history, so they aren't a good option if you'd like to have a conventional bank account again, but they have their advantages. They don't require a credit check or a squeaky clean banking history. However, they may have transaction fees, ATM fees, balance requirements, and may lack features like online banking. Nerdwallet.com is a great resource to compare prepaid debit cards.

Improving your credit score

So maybe you checked your credit score and found that it's in the lower end of the scale. Or maybe you have already experienced the frustration of being denied after applying for a credit card. There are no quick fixes in improving your credit scores, but there are lots of steps you can take to improve it over time.

Here are some long-term good habits to improve your credit score: Pay bills on time, pay off debt, keep balances within 30% of your credit limit across all cards, apply for new credit accounts only as needed, don't close unused credit cards, and dispute any inaccuracies on your credit reports.

There are a few more immediate short-term solutions. Experian, one of the three major credit reporting agencies, has a service called Experian Boost which inputs data from paying your utilities and mobile phone bills towards your score (normally they aren't counted). Another option is asking to be an authorized user on the account of someone with good credit who trusts you, like a spouse or parent. This essentially gives you your own card, but the responsibility for the charges go to the main card holder. Even if you personally don't make charges on the account, their good credit card habits will still have a positive effect on your credit score.

Getting your first credit card to improve your credit score

If you have a low credit score because you've never had a credit card, it might be time to apply for an account. You don't have to switch over to paying everything with plastic to get a bump to your score. Here's a simple step by step:

- Research credit cards for 30 minutes (nerdwallet.com and bankrates.com are great comparison tools).

- Pick one that is likely to approve your credit score range and apply. If you don't get approved, it's okay, wait a month and apply to a different one.

- Set up a single, monthly expense to be billed on it. It can be as small as just a Netflix or Spotify account. So long as it's monthly, and you know you'll be able to pay in full each month

- Set up your credit card to automatically collect the full monthly payment from your checking account.

- (if needed) To keep from spending too much on your new credit card, hide it somewhere in your home. Freeze it in a block of ice, if you really want to amp up the drama.

Doing this will prove your ability to pay monthly bills on time and grow the length of your credit history, two of the factors that make up your credit score.

Getting a credit card account when you have a bad credit score

If you have a low credit score, have tried applying for a few regular credit cards in your credit range, and have still been denied, a secured credit card may help you. The difference between a secured credit card and a standard one is that you make a cash deposit when you open the account, usually the limit on the credit card, normally at least $200. They have a benefit of repairing your credit, given that you use the card sparingly (1-2 purchases a month) and pay the balance in full every month. But even this method can take a year to improve your score to the point that you could apply for or transfer to a regular credit card. It's always a slow slog with credit building, unfortunately.

If your debts are too much to handle

If you are looking at your minimum payments and it's just not adding up, there are additional options. They may not fit your situation, but this is the rock bottom.

- Still negotiate! See if the creditors can work with you in any way on lowering the monthly rate. They'd rather get paid a little than nothing at all, so there may be flexibility if you ask for it.

- Look into the interest rates of personal loans at your bank. (If the interest rate is higher than a credit card would be, they aren't a good option)

- Ask a friend or family member for help or a loan.

- Online donations through GoFundMe. Nearly 250,000 campaigns have been set up through the site to help pay for healthcare costs, raising $650 million in contributions, according to the company's website. One third of all donations on the site go to healthcare costs. Maybe not the right option for your situation, but one that has presented itself as a way to fundraise online in recent times.

- Counterproductive, but if your only other option is a payday loan, put it on a credit card instead. Payday loans are evil, remember?

And if this list still leaves you at a loss, consider seeking help from a professional, a financial advocate specializing in debt management. A good debt management organization can work with creditors on your behalf and help you make a plan to be debt free within 3-5 years. Debt settlement, while sounding similar, is far riskier. They attempt to negotiate down your total debt balance, but there are additional fees and taxes, and no guarantees the creditors will be on board, potentially leaving you worse off than you started. Another option is bankruptcy, but it is one of the most serious financial decisions you can make. It's legally being discharged of debt and getting a fresh start. However, your assets may be liquidated, your wages garnished, and it'll be on your record for 7-10 years. Also, often child support, taxes, and student loans aren't eligible for forgiveness in bankruptcy. For more information on debt management (and to explore if bankruptcy is right for you), you can visit the National Foundation for Credit Counseling at www.nfcc.org or call at 800-388-2227.

Recovering from Financial Abuse

While financial abuse can mean crimes like bank fraud and forged signatures, I'd like to briefly address financial abuse within a personal relationship. Financial abuse is a common tactic used by abusers to gain power and control in a relationship; 90% of domestic abuse survivors experience a form of financial abuse. This could manifest as abusers controlling a victim's ability to earn income or maintain their own bank accounts, or as a caregiver misusing an elderly person's financial resources. For dependent, college-bound youths, this could be an abusive parent limiting their access to money or loans.

If you are experiencing financial abuse, there are steps to reclaiming your independence. Safety is the most important thing, and planning your way out in advance can reduce your risk. Start by gathering information: phone numbers and addresses of trusted friends, contacts related to your children, and domestic shelters in your area you could access in an emergency. Gather documentation of your situation (if accessible): bank statements, pay stubs, tax forms, birth and marriage certificates, lease/mortgage, credit card and utility bills. Store all these documents with a trusted friend, outside of your own home. Make an exit strategy: where you will go (friends, family, a hotel, a shelter) and how you will get there (transport). Based on your exit plan, calculate how much money you'll need (housing, food, travel costs, etc.) It may not be possible to openly save money in a financial abuse situation, so you'll need to find covert ways to put together the funds, potentially selling possessions, doing cash back when grocery shopping and hiding it, starting a side job, or asking your support system for funds. Once you've secured funds and a place to go, take your leave. You can explain to your employer, file for temporary support, get a restraining order, and contact any joint financial institutions once you are safely out of the home. This is not a blanket solution by any means, but it's a framework for seeing a way out.

These are especially difficult situations, but there are organizations that aid in finding a way through: For domestic relationships: U.S. National Domestic Violence Hotline; 1-800-799-7233 and nnedv.org. For elder abuse: National Center on Elder Abuse, 1-855-500-3537 ncea.acl. gov.

When your income is just too low to afford living costs

The minimum estimated income required to secure the necessities of life is what is called the "poverty line". The poverty guideline is a set of income thresholds, defined by the U.S. government (Department of Health and Human Services), to decide who is and is not in poverty and is dependent on the size and income of a household. As of January 2020, the poverty guideline for a single person is an income of $12,760. In 2018, 38.1 million people lived below the poverty guideline; that's 11.8% of Americans. Even more dismally, one in five children in the United States live in poverty.

Since 2009, the federal minimum wage has remained at $7.25 an hour, but there are exceptions to this at the state and city levels. If you worked 40-hour weeks, every week, for the entire year, your annual salary on the federal minimum wage would be $15,080. This puts a single individual just above the poverty guideline, but a single parent making that wage would be considered below the poverty threshold. The government does have several social aid programs in place to assist those with low income. Each is dedicated to aid in a certain aspect of life, such as food, housing, and healthcare. I've provided information on what they are, who qualifies, and where to apply in the back of this book.

And more

This is just a small collection of the unfortunate pitfalls of personal finance. Each of the topics in this chapter have additional complexities, and there are so many more roadblocks and challenges I didn't mention. In the next chapter I'll cover some ways to safeguard yourself from getting into these situations to begin with.

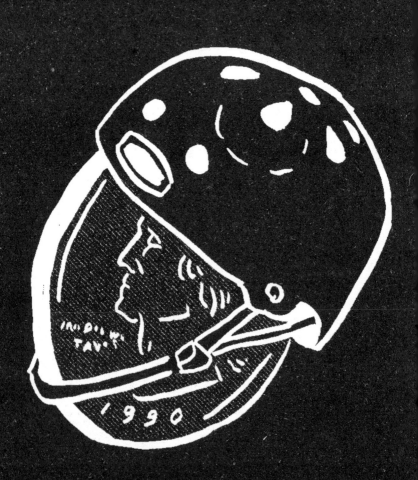

8

PROTECTING MONEY

We've worked through the basics of staying balanced with money: income, spending, budgeting. We've learned about the importance of saving for the future. But even the most financially savvy person would only get so far if a really devastating (and expensive) emergency occurred; a serious health crisis, natural disasters, horrible accidents. Incidents that can completely ruin you financially. That's where an often maligned concept comes in: insurance.

Insurance at its most basic is a financial product that you pay for on an annual or monthly basis, and should a costly incident occur, they will help you by paying some or all of the costs. They come in lots of genres: health, life, home, even pets. Generally speaking, the best case scenario with having any insurance is that you never have to use it, because that means nothing bad has happened that would necessitate you to use the coverage. No one got sick or experienced a car accident, great! But it can feel counterintuitive to pay for something you ideally never utilize. Try to think of it as a safety net. Living life is inherently a tightrope act, but no matter how great an acrobat you may be, it's comforting to know if you fell, you'd be okay.

Some insurances to prioritize

Health Insurance: To help cover medical costs, especially in the event of a health crisis. This insurance is the most important for an individual to have, but it's also incredibly complex. In the United States, you can acquire health insurance either through your employer or through the federal government. The government offers health insurance through the ACA healthcare market, also known as Obamacare, as well as through Medicaid for those of low income and Medicare for those over 65.

To start, you pay a monthly fee called a premium to have the insurance. The plan will have a minimum amount you will pay for medical expenses out of your own pocket before the insurance company pays anything, and that's called the deductible. Once you've spent enough to meet the deductible, your insurance will cover part or all medical costs (although you still continue to pay the monthly premium). Another factor into picking a plan is the group of doctors and hospitals your insurance has included in its coverage, which is called a "network." Each insurance plan negotiates different flat rates (co-pays) and percentage costs (co-insurance) for different procedures, although it's complicated to know exactly how much you can expect to pay given the opaque billing practices and murkiness about who exactly is in-network.

In the past 20 years, the cost of medical care has absolutely skyrocketed. That in turn inflates the cost of health insurance premiums, which has become a hardship for many. Upwards of 44 million Americans go uninsured, not only exposing them to financial risk, but also health risk; it's likely they aren't getting regular healthcare at all for fear of what it may cost. The number one cause of personal bankruptcy is medical expenses, yet the even more jarring fact is that many of those filers had some sort of health insurance.

None of that is inspiring, but ultimately, having health insurance is still important. Your health is a precious asset, and access to care is critical. Many preventative care visits and treatments are free (within your network) by law: STI screening, lots of immunizations, well-woman visits, and more. While the current healthcare market is beyond unjust, prioritizing health insurance and, more importantly, your health, is crucial.

Homeowners / Renters Insurance: To help cover events of theft or disaster. Most mortgage lenders will require you to have homeowners insurance to cover your home, your personal property, and liability. The most common coverage includes coverage for fire, theft, windstorms, freezing of plumbing, among a set list of others.

If you rent, your landlord is required to pay for repairs on the building in the event of a fire or burst pipe, but not on any damage to your belongings or if someone is injured in the rental. Renters insurance covers your possessions and some liability in those events. Your landlord may or may not require you to have a renters insurance policy. Further, some landlords will require a specific amount of liability coverage. Even if your landlord doesn't have requirements on renters insurance, it is a smart move to get it. Luckily, it's pretty affordable, around $15 a month.

Car Insurance: To help cover if you are involved in a collision or other covered incidents, like theft or fire. Every state but New Hampshire requires vehicle owners to have some amount of car insurance liability coverage, which has three components: bodily injury coverage per person, bodily injury coverage per accident, and property damage coverage per accident. It's often written as a set of numbers like 25/50/20 for example, meaning your coverage would pay up to $25,000 per person for bodily injuries caused to people in a car you hit but no more than $50,000 in total bodily injury costs for the incident. You'd also be covered for up to $20,000 in property damage.

In addition to liability, about 40% of states require uninsured/underinsured motorist coverage, which protects you if you are hit by someone driving without insurance or with too little insurance to cover the injuries to you or your passengers. A few states also require uninsured property damage.

About 20% states additionally require personal injury protection (PIP) which covers your—or your passengers'—injuries, no matter who is at fault in an accident. Depending on the policy, this can cover medical bills, rehabilitation, and income loss.

No state requires collision and comprehensive coverage, but these are common add-ons that help with car thefts, animal collisions, and more. There are other options like medical payments coverage, rental reimbursement, roadside assistance, towing, and full glass coverage.

It can be tempting to purchase just the minimum rates required by your state to save money, but the minimums aren't realistically enough to cover you in an accident, and can have costly consequences. If you are in an accident with the lowest possible coverage, you are 100% responsible for the expenses that exceed the state minimum car insurance coverage. If you don't have enough cash to pay the difference, the other driver has grounds to sue you and potentially claim your assets or have your wages garnished. It can flip your life upside-down.

Determining the right amount of car insurance is tricky, especially with factors like location, age, and car model affecting the rates available to you. Most insurers recommend having 100/300/50 coverage instead of the state minimum to realistically cover you financially if you are in an accident. If you are leasing or financing a car, you will likely be required to carry collision coverage and comprehensive coverage as well, although these may be considered optional if you own the car outright.

The good news is that you can shop around for this coverage with relative ease to find a competitive rate for the coverage you need. There also may be discounts for safe drivers and bundling policies with home owner or renters insurance.

Life Insurance: To provide money to dependents in the event of your own death. Life insurance is a good safety net for those with children or if you have someone who is financially dependent on your income. Costs vary by age, gender, and how much coverage you need. Policy amount ranges between $250,000 to $1,000,000 and may be intended to cover the funeral, replace your income, pay off the mortgage and/or send your kid to college. There's also the choice between term or whole. Term policies are a set number of decades and less expensive. Whole is your entire life and is more expensive, but has a cash value at the end, whereas term does not.

Long Term Disability Insurance: To help cover an inability to work (and therefore earn income) due to an injury or illness for a long period of time (1-2+ years). The incident doesn't have to happen at your job to be covered, and can help keep you afloat while unable to work by compensating you a percentage (typically 50-70%) of your salary for a set number of years. Many employers offer this for free or at a discount, and it's worth having just in case. A note on short term disability: for the most part skip it, unless you are eminently planning to get pregnant. It's expensive, and as long as you have an emergency fund to cover 3 months expenses, long term disability would kick in after that.

Insurances that you may want to (critically) consider

There are lots of types of insurance out there; fear of the future extends far and wide. But the key to determining if they are worth paying for is comparing the cost of what exactly they cover, and just as importantly, what they exclude. Be sure you understand what you're buying before you commit, read the fine print, and call them if you have questions.

Dental and Vision Insurance: It's worth noting that health insurance doesn't usually include dental or vision services, and while I wouldn't blanket recommend against having coverage, they may end up costing more than just paying out of pocket. Dental insurance typically has a maximum benefit, which means even after paying a monthly premium and a deductible, they have a limit of how much they'll pay for in a given year. Whether you are expecting only to do your normal check ups, or anticipate pricier procedures, it's worth calling your dentist and asking what you'd be charged without insurance and compare that with the combined costs of the dental insurance deductible, premium, and percentage of visits they would cover. Vision insurance may be something to consider if you require more frequent exams (family history of eye disease, diabetes diagnosis, older age, etc.).

For those who only need routine eye exams, it may be less costly to do those visits out of pocket.

Private Mortgage Insurance: If you purchase a home without a downpayment of at least 20% you may be required to have PMI. This protects the bank against loss when lending to a high-risk borrower. You pay for this insurance, but all protections are for the bank. If you're able to wait until you have a full down payment, you aren't required to carry this insurance.

Pet Insurance: This helps cover accidents and unforeseen illnesses of cats and dogs. Typically, it doesn't include routine check ups, vaccinations, or medications (unless you opt into a wellness add-on to your policy). Most policies have waiting periods, so you can't just sign up after an incident occurs and expect coverage. Many conditions that pets are born with or are hereditary won't be covered. Some plans even have an age cap. Given all these exclusions, if you feel your pet is at a high risk for accident or illness like poisoning or infection, you'll want to examine sample policies from the insurer. Overall, it may be a better deal to use what you would have spent on premiums towards an emergency fund just for your pet.

Travel Insurance: There are many a la carte options for coverage you can purchase around travel: protection against lost bags, cancelled trips, insurance for a rental car, out of network medical expenses. However, you'll want to check to see if your other insurances potentially cover you in these situations (home, life, auto, and health insurances). For example, a credit card may offer a perk of coverage for lost luggage or theft. But travel insurance can be helpful if the coverage you already have falls short. For instance, Medicaid provides no option for healthcare coverage outside of the United States.

Home Warranties: Not technically insurance, but often gets lumped in. It's more like a service contract. It can cover things like your stove, air conditioning, plumbing, and other home appliances defined in the policy. If you need a repair, they charge a service fee to come evaluate the issue, and they may determine it falls outside the policy because the appliance has too much wear and tear or it's installed incorrectly. Even if they do repair it, the warranty may only cover a fraction of the cost. There are lots of gaps in expectations for home warranties, and many people decide to put away money in a savings fund for repairs.

Insurances that are basically scams

Identity theft insurance: There are federal laws in place to protect you from being liable for credit card charges made fraudulently. Most credit cards already offer complete protection. This insurance won't prevent your identity from being stolen, but pays for expenses incurred in reclaiming your identity, like attorney fees and lost wages. However, the best thing is for you to monitor your debit and credit accounts and report any mysterious charges as soon as you see them.

Children's life insurance: This sounds calloused, but unless the family depends on the child's income, there's no need to have this insurance.

Rental car insurance: If you have full auto insurance on a vehicle you own, you probably are covered with rentals, but it's worth double checking. If you don't own a car, your credit card may also cover it if you pay for the rental with that card. Same goes for car rental damage insurance. Be sure to check your car insurance or credit card benefit coverage before you rent.

Extended Warranties on individual products: These warranties are designed to end before the product realistically will have an issue, maybe a year or two. They sure are profitable for stores though!

And many more: Flight insurance, accidental death insurance, disease insurance, mortgage life insurance, and credit card insurance are all likely to be covered by an existing insurance you carry, or typically have narrow uses. Probably avoidable!

Shopping for insurance

You can and should shop for insurance policies like any other financial product. Some of the variables to consider when comparing policies are:

How much and what kind of coverage you need

For instance, if you're looking at renter's insurance, that would involve estimating the worth of all your possessions (insurers often have calculators to help you with this). With car insurance, it may be 100/30/50 and any additional state required coverage. For health insurance, maybe it's a specific doctor you need in-network.

What premiums you can afford

The premium is the annual or monthly fee you pay for the coverage. Generally, the higher your premium, the lower your deductible. If you were shopping for health insurance, and you have a chronic illness, you may want to opt for a plan with a higher premium and a lower deductible if you know you'll reach your deductible within the year.

Where you want to set your deductible

A deductible is the amount of money you have to spend out of pocket (in addition to your monthly premium) before the insurance kicks in to cover anything. Generally, the higher your deductible, the lower your premium. If you were shopping for health insurance and you were in relatively good health, you may want to opt for a plan with a lower premium and a high deductible, since your risk will be lower than you'll actually need to use the insurance.

I can sympathize that insurance can feel like you're throwing money into a big old pit, never to be seen again. But it stings even worse if something unfortunate does happen, and you have no backstop or assistance with the bills.

I want to impress upon you that without these insurances, you open yourself up to a lot of risk; risk that something devastating may happen to you, your home, your livelihood, or your loved one that could leave you in dire straits financially, in addition to dealing with a huge crisis. Insurance won't prevent bad things from happening, but it will help ease the blow of bearing the entire financial responsibility of crises that can range in cost from a few thousand to a few hundred thousand dollars. It's really meant to be a backstop on the expenses when the worst of the worst things happen.

So while, financially speaking, insurance is a good way of protecting your money, there are other aspects of protection that are important as well: taking care of your body and being supported by your community.

Your community

Our society has a very individualistic bent, but there is still truth to the old axiom of "strength in numbers." Knowing your neighbors sounds like a cheesy old timey thing in the age of the internet, but it's really true. If you get locked out of the house, it's cheaper to call a neighbor than a locksmith. When you're out of town, it's nice to know that someone is keeping an eye on things for you. Your larger social community of friends and family can be a godsend when you need a recommendation for a plumber, a babysitter when your child is sick, or you want to borrow a food processor. There are lots of local "buy nothing groups" online and you can search for your town or neighborhood, or start one yourself! Other local efforts could be setting up a babysitting co-op among your parent friends, or even setting up a free lending library in your community. Building strong, lasting relationships not only is another layer of support in crisis, but also engenders emotional, social, professional, spiritual, mental, and, yes, financial health.

9

INVESTING MONEY

Ah investing. That topic that polarizes the population into enthusiasts and skeptics. I'd like you to set aside any feelings or preconceived notions you have of investing. It's a healthy part of any financial plan, and something that everyone should do, not just people who wear monocles.

Investing is simply putting money into financial products that can potentially generate more money by increasing in value, typically over a long period of time, at different levels of risk. Some examples of investing are running a business, renting a property you own, a retirement fund, and stocks. Making money by investing in the financial markets through stocks, bonds, and indexes isn't guaranteed, but over many years, the gains have historically outweighed the losses. This can start to seem like it's overly complicated, risky, and not for you, but let me try and change your mind. Investing can be a "set it and forget it" thing, and it really is an essential step in long term financial wellbeing.

Before we dive in

This chapter will break down what investing is, why it's important, and how to get started. While investing is a key part of long term planning, it shouldn't come at the expense of more foundational steps, like managing your debt and having some savings. It's simply a better value for your money to pay off credit card debit before aggressively investing. It's also important to keep some cash in savings for quick access in an emergency. So before you begin your adventures in investing, it's smart to be in a stable financial position first:

- Pay off your high interest debts (nothing with an interest rate over 8% or so)

- Save a good sized emergency fund (~1-3 month's worth of expenses)

When I got into personal finance, it took me several years to get to a point that I was able to invest at all. I encourage you to invest as soon as you responsibly can, but personal financial health is a long haul. While it may take some time, you'll have more success focusing on the step right in front of you than all the steps you have to go.

What is investing?

Investing is a tried and true practice of having your money make money for you. You may think of investing as the chaos of the stock market and aggressive hedge funds, and yes, that's part of it, but for 99% of us, that isn't the type of investing we would benefit from. Yep, we're talking about the boring kind: building wealth over decades to use after you've decided to retire from employment.

Typically, in America, people are eligible to retire from working around 62 years of age. This is when you can start collecting Social Security, the federal retirement program we all pay into automatically via a tax on our income (go on, check your pay stub, remember?). On average, Americans live to be around 78 years old. So, that would be 16 years of living without an income from a job. The amount you receive from social security depends on your age when you begin to collect benefits and your income level when you did work. As of June 2018, the average Social Security retirement benefit paid to a retired worker is $1,413 per month, or just about $17,000 a year. Not a lot of dough.

This is where personal retirement savings come in. As you know by now, saving money is super important to get the things you want in life, and isn't a comfortable standard of living in your golden years something you want? It may seem far away, but the reason that retirement savings should be treated with a sense of urgency is that investments, over time, snowball into a larger sum than if you just sacked it away under your mattress. Now allow me a moment of silliness in a bit of a drab chapter, and to sing you a lymric from the third act of the 1957 classic film Mary Poppins: "if you invest your tuppence wisely in the bank, safe and sound, soon that tuppences safely invested in the bank, will compound."

Compound interest!

In addition to songs, I have some pictures to entertain and delight you. Here we have three graphs. Each is a universe where you save $50 a month, every month, for

30 years. But where you put that money you save can be the difference of **tens of thousands of dollars.**

Example 1: cash jar

Let's say you put a crisp $50 bill in a jar every month for 30 years. You will have a total of **$18,000**! Not a bad chunk of change. However, this is also in a world where you never dip into that jar in times of need, and it never gets stolen. It's pretty risky to simply have cash just laying around in a big jar, but like I said, best case scenario: $18,000 in cash.

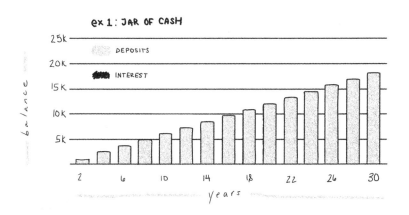

Example 2: savings account

Okay, so you're a little bit more savvy and you forego the cash jar. You take that same $50 a month you'd be saving, and you set up an automatic monthly transfer for

$50 from your checking account to your savings account. Let's say that your savings account is currently getting a 2% interest rate (and that it stays 2% into the future). Every month, the bank will pay you 2% of your total balance, just for being their customer. So after the first month you'd have $50+$1=$51. The second month you'd have $50+$51+$2.01= $103.01 and so on. You see how it's not just 2% of every 50 dollars deposited, but 2% of the total sum? This is what it means for interest to compound. So, after 30 years of saving $50 a month, every month, without dipping in ever, with this 2% interest, your total would be *$24,636*. Without saving any more than you would in the first example, just by using a savings account instead of a jar, *you'll have made an additional $6,636 in pure interest payments from the bank!*

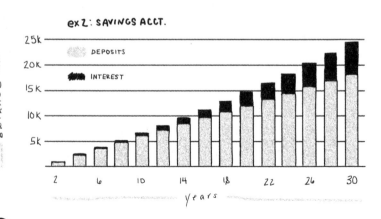

ex 2: SAVINGS ACCT.

Example 3: investing

Alright, maybe by this point you're on to me. It's abundantly clear that a savings account is better than the sock drawer, but let's look at how much money you'd end up with if you put $50 a month, every month, into a retirement investment account, such as a 401(k) or Roth IRA, which typically returns 10% (although this can and does fluctuate, with the benefit of time, it averages out to 10%). So, in this example, when you're ready to retire, just like the other two, you would have put $18,000 of your own money into the account. However, due to the high compound interest rate of investments, your account would hold *$113,024.*

That's $95,024 dollars that was purely interest on your deposits. 95k you would have missed out on by digging a hole in your yard, and 81K you would have missed out on if you simply parked it in a savings account. That is right. That is why people write songs in children's movies about investing.

It's a little easier to see in the graphs, but you are wanting to see a big, dramatic curve up, not just a steady upward trajectory. Compound interest is what brings in that curve, and investing will give you the most dramatic returns on your retirement savings.

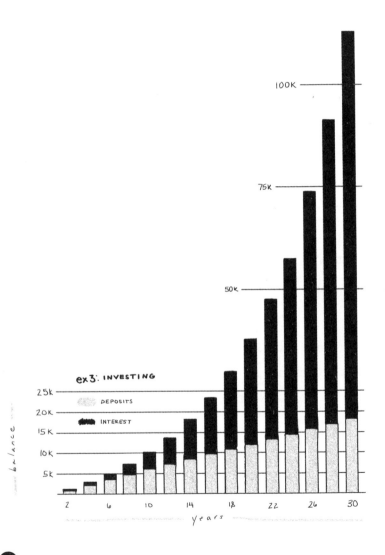

ex 3. INVESTING

DEPOSITS
INTEREST

balance

years

Another facet of compound interest is the aspect of time. The nature of compound interest basically means a higher rate of return the longer you wait. In this 3rd example, you can see the huge gains in those last 2 years are the biggest gains of all.

Just a note on the graphs: There is another factor at play in these 3 projections—inflation. Inflation is the rate at which money becomes more or less valuable in the global economy. In your grandma's day, she could buy a coke for a nickel; in your mother's day, she could buy one for a quarter, and you can buy one for about a dollar. The generally accepted inflation rate will slightly devalue your money over time, roughly 2-3%. So maybe your daughter's coke will cost $1.50. An unavoidable bummer to be sure, but something to note with these long projections.

The investment ladder

So, let's say you're free of high interest debt and you have a healthy emergency fund saved. Congrats! You're doing great, and you are ready for the next step. Speaking of steps, a great tool to thinking about investing strategy is a ladder, a metaphor coined by financial writer Ramit Sethi.

Each step of the investing ladder builds on the previous one, and gives a clear path of where to go next. Being on the bottom rung of this ladder is already a really big accomplishment.

Anyway, the ladder:

- Rung 1: Take full advantage of your employer's 401(k) match, if offered.

  - As mentioned in the savings chapter, a 401(k) is an investment savings account an employer may offer. They may deposit money in themselves, and you can put money into it directly from your salary before taxes. When you're 59.5, you can start taking money out of the account. Plan on not touching that money until you're ready to retire, as withdrawals before the minimum age will have a tax penalty.

  - A 401(k) match is when an employer offers to deposit additional funds in the account for you, "matching" the amount you yourself deposit. Let's say they do a 3% match on your 50K salary. Each month, $125 of your pay, before taxes, goes into the 401(k) account, and your employer deposits an additional $125 into your account (free money!). If you have your debt and emergency fund under control, and can manage the savings for the match, you absolutely should do it.

- ○ Just a note on taxes and 401(k)s: because you invest your income before it's taxed, you do pay taxes when you make withdrawals in retirement.

- ○ If your employer doesn't have a 401(k) or doesn't offer to deposit or match any funds for you, bummer, skip the 401(k) for now, and move onto rung 2.

- Rung 2: Pay off any high and medium interest debts

  - ○ Paying off debt actually is an investment in that you are eliminating the cost of the interest payments. Focus all your resources on eliminating debts that carry a big percentage. Getting rid of this burden is a significant instant return.

- The debts that you could have and responsibly move onto rung 3 would be low interest car loans, home loans, or student debt, but anything over 3% should be prioritized to be paid off.

- Rung 3: Open a Roth IRA and contribute as much as you can to it.

  - This is similar to a 401(k) in that it's an investment savings account, but instead of depositing from your paycheck pretax, you deposit from your checking account after tax. The advantage is that withdrawals in retirement are tax-free, and you also have more control over what you'd want to invest in.

  - The difference between a Roth IRA and a Traditional IRA (along with 401(k)s, usually) is that with a traditional IRA you get a tax break now, but pay taxes when you withdraw in retirement, where with a Roth IRA you pay the taxes now, and you withdraw tax free in retirement. Over the long term, for most people, the Roth is the better deal.

- In 2019, the max you could deposit a year was $6,000. Even if you put just $50 a month into it, it's better there than your savings account if you can spare it.

- Also, if you have medium term goals (a new car, a down payment on a home, preparing for a baby) consider those as seperate savings goals alongside your investment effort.

- While there is a bit of flexibility on withdrawing from a Roth IRA before you retire, plan on not touching your Roth IRA deposits till retirement.

- Rung 4: If you've maxed out your Roth IRA and still have money you want to invest, then invest more in the 401(k).

  - Alright, first off, if you are at this step, *congrats*. You are able to set aside $500 each month for your Roth IRA? Not impossible, but incredibly commendable. Sorry, I just had to say it.

  - Once you've met the limit for your Roth IRA, you can still contribute to that 401(k) in addition to any match the company offers you. For 2019, that max is $19K a year.

- Rung 5: Still have money to invest after maxing that out? Open a regular non-retirement investment account and invest it there.

  ○ If you're on this rung, literally why are you reading this book? But really, there are lots of resources out there for you, and if you're on rung 4 or 5, you have officially outpaced this book.

Other Investment Products

Some investment vocab we have not touched in this chapter are: stocks, money markets, bonds, ETFs, mutual funds, bitcoin, IPOs, options, CDs, annuities, commissions, and so on.

To be honest, their exclusion is intentional. Many of them are relegated to Rung 5, when you've maxed out your tax advantaged retirement accounts. And even at rung 5, the best advice I can offer is do not put your money into something you don't understand, and if you have questions, seek out a financial professional who is a fiduciary (someone who is bound ethically to act in your best interests, not to just sell you things).

However, in lieu of a breakdown of the complex details of all your independent investing options, I have a few golden rules of investing:

Passive investing is the best investing

The less human intervention you have on your investments, the better. Ideally, you would only glance at your account once a quarter. I fully give you permission to ignore stock pickers and financial forecasting as far as investments go because actively managed funds, whether by you or a professional, have rarely proven to outperform the market. I can't stress it enough: it actually is a great move to set and forget a balanced investment account.

Index Funds are your friends

When you're looking at your 401(k) or Roth IRA account, and you have to decide what vehicle your deposits get invested in, an index fund is a perfect option. An index fund is a single product that is made up of a collection of stocks, bonds, real estate investments, etc. They come in lots of combinations, but the main point is that the fund is diversified, meaning it has many different kinds of investments, not just one, so in case one part of the portfolio performed terribly, you won't lose your entire investment.

For a 401(k) you'll be picking from whatever funds your company provides, but for a Roth IRA, you can choose where to set up your account. Firms like Vanguard and Fidelity both offer index funds that have pretty low fees and are industry strongholds. A current trend in investment vehicles are "robo" advisors websites like Betterment and Wealthfront. Because algorithms manage the funds, not people with salaries, fees are low and there's little risk of human intervention. Ultimately you want something with low fees, and a proportional mix of investment types for your age.

Change your portfolio ratios as you age

Typically, you want to balance the investments in your portfolio with different levels of risk. When you're young, you have the benefit of time to make up any big losses and capitalize on big gains, so you should have more high risk/high reward investments like stocks in your index fund. When you're older, you don't want to risk losing too much, so it's advised to take on more low risk/low reward investments like bonds in your index fund. A typical rule of thumb is that 100 minus your age is the percentage of stocks you should have in your fund; however, some advise 110 or 120 minus age, as people are living longer these days.

Do not touch your retirement fund before you retire
Not to help out your family, not to pay for your child's school, just don't. This is absolutely an oxygen mask on the airplane type situation: you have to take care of yourself before you can help others.

Investing has such a bad rap but it's simply a tool, a tool for generating money incrementally over time. It may seem like a lot to soak in, and it kind of is. Humans are not innately good at fathoming long periods of time, big numbers, or risk. However, the best thing you can do is simply open your 401(k) or Roth IRA account and make a small recurring deposit. Remember, even $50 can get you tens of thousands in interest down the road. Trust me, your future self will be so happy you did.

10

GIVING MONEY

One aspect of personal finance I think is woefully under reported is giving money to people and causes you believe in.

If you're reading this book, it's likely that you are cognizant of the oppressive power of both capitalism and consumerism, as well as the prevalence of financial inequality. And I'm also guessing you champion organizations and people that are working to improve our world. In America especially, there is an individualistic mentality: the money you make goes toward the life you want to lead. Money also acts as security, and can evoke a hoarding mentality. I grew up with a culture of being very frugal and squirreling away money because *You Never Know*. And this is something that many personal finance writers also promote. While it's a great goal to be safe, secure, prepared for anything, there are also rewards to paying it forward.

Pop psychology has brought this concept to the forefront: helping others leads to high levels of "happiness." While the research can be a bit casual, there are undeniable motivations for altruism: from your own wellbeing, to social signalling, to tax breaks. Whatever your reasons are, you can absolutely plan these into your budget, or make it a goal to be able to do so. And just like some enjoy shopping around different stores for items, you can apply that same logic to learning about charities, both national and local. If you brainstorm the values you hold, there's sure to be organizations of all sizes dedicated to those causes: food scarcity, local journalism, LGBTQ+ resources, youth programing, abolition groups, animal protection, the environment, human rights. You can always start small; $5 a month can still make a difference.

Another way to approach giving is with your time. Your community undoubtedly has organizations you already support and sometimes they need a dependable volunteer more than they do a one time donation. A pair of hands can be taught; your time and attention are impactful resources. If you are a designer, an accountant, or simply willing to show up, you may find that offering your skills is worth as much to an organization as your funds.

Part of my personal finance journey has very much been scrutinizing the organizations I give my money too, not only donation wise, but commercially as well. A great way to start looking at this for yourself is looking at your spending log. Are there purchases you made at a national chain that could have been made locally? Or maybe you could take something you buy frequently, like coffee or cosmetics, and seek out an independent company to try, maybe even prioritizing businesses owned by women or people of color. For evaluating companies on their political, environmental, and ethical standing, you can use websites like grabyourwallet.org, ethicalconsumer. org, and goodonyou.eco. Consider sending some money to artists you've enjoyed for free online via Patreon, Ko-fi, Bandcamp, or buying something directly from their online shop. For the past few years, I've made donations to charities during the holidays in lieu of gifts for extended family. On a larger scale, I don't own a car, and that's in part because of my concern over climate change. There's lots of opportunity to be creative and intentional in where your money goes.

A delicate situation presents itself when a family member or friend is in need of help. It can often feel great when you are able to give a financial gift to someone you love in a time of need. A slightly stickier sensation is when someone asks you for money as a loan, promising to pay you back. This can immediately cause a strain on the relationship, but it's not impossible to navigate. The best advice I've heard for this is: give that money as a gift— don't expect that money back. If you cannot afford for them not to repay you, you simply can't afford to do it. If you are able to afford the sum they are asking for, offer it as a one time gift, with a caveat: if they repay it in full, then you'd be open to loaning to them again. If they aren't able to repay you, you should be clear you won't be able to give them any further money. This way you're clear on the expectations, while allowing yourself to ward off resentment on not being repaid.

And to wrap up, if you aren't in a position to afford charitable giving, or giving your time, that is okay. If you're not taking care of you, you're not in a position to help anyone else. There will always be more need than any one of us can fulfill. You can always show up in ways that don't have a price tag.

11

IN CLOSING

The conventional path to financial stability is clear: get income, spend less than you earn, be aware of your spending, get out of debt, create an emergency fund, be insured, invest in your future, and give back. Listed in this way it sounds deceivingly straightforward. In reality, that path can have many twists, turns, and potholes. Some can run it, some may need to walk, others require a hand to get out of the mud. I'm alluding to privilege, circumstance, and luck. But the path remains more or less the same; these are the basic hallmarks of money management.

A firm understanding of personal finance is certainly important, however it's just one aspect of who you are. There are several other facets to life that make up your wellbeing: physical, nutritional, emotional, social, spiritual, intellectual, and occupational. These dimensions overlap and influence one another, affecting your health and quality of life. Working on your financial situations may be taxing on other aspects of your wellbeing at first, but with practice, it will get easier.

When I started learning about personal finance, it was frustrating and sometimes brought me to tears. Digesting the totality of my student debt alongside rent and an entry level job left me feeling like I'd be in this purgatory forever. After some time, I started to see the progress I had made, and it felt easier to face. Over months and years, I found better jobs, started saving, and began to think of the future. Managing my money shifted from a burden into something that empowered me. When I divorced money from fear and shame, it allowed me to think about what I actually want in life, and the confidence to reach for it. And not just in a financial way; understanding my values changed the jobs I pursue, the volunteer opportunities I participate in, the food I eat, the kind of partner I am to my spouse, and the everyday choices I make day to day.

The best life money can buy is not one of immense wealth; it's one where you feel healthy, hopeful, content with your job, and secure in your ability to weather life's inevitable blows. One where you've cultivated meaningful interests and strong relationships. One where money is separate from who you are, but affords you a life worth living.

And Yet

This book was written for the most part before the coronavirus pandemic, and while the tactical advice in this book still stands, this crisis may finally force a change in how the issue of financial inequality is addressed in our society.

Setting aside the horrors of the disease itself, the pandemic response in America caused the economy to atrophy and millions to lose their jobs. As of this writing, one in six workers isn't currently employed. Without income, securing the basic necessities of food, housing, and medical care is a hardship. And while these issues were already widespread pre-pandemic, we can no longer blame the victims of inequality with the fallacy of "not trying hard enough."

The American Dream posits that anyone can succeed if they work hard and play by the rules. In the first chapter we covered that this isn't true, but the concept has endured. It's the gleaming facade of a culture that centers on privatization, not just in an economic sense, but on a social level as well. Private life and private satisfaction are heralded as the pinnacle of existence; you are solely responsible for your own success, and you are entitled to those rewards, and to protect them, if you end up successful. This mindset seals us all into our own individual silos. When it's generally accepted that you and you alone are responsible for your success and failures, it allows any notion of collective concern or collective power to wither. This translates to the dismantling of unions and societal safety nets. This system has created massive advantages for the wealthy, enshrining them into law, leaving the rest of us to "pull ourselves up by our bootstraps."

However, disasters tend to shake loose the old orders. A collective shift towards equality has been seen in previous moments of crisis—resiliency and generosity spring forth, independent of leadership. Whether it's an earthquake, flood, or pandemic, people tend to forego the private concern for the civic. Disasters can shift our priorities from just ourselves to the shared needs of the community: access to housing, food, education, safety, wages, and medical care. These are massive systemic issues in "normal" times, but a crisis can reveal the extent by which our government fails to protect us. At the same time, in these moments of shared suffering and sacrifice, a crisis can tap into our innate desire as individuals for connection and purposefulness. Suddenly, it's made clear what we have in common: that we all deserve safety and support, and it's possible to make it happen ourselves.

You can see this clearly in recent times with the proliferation of mutual aid groups, from meal kits to childcare collectives to funds for rent, all popping up without a top-down leader orchestrating or funding these efforts. The pandemic underscored the existing need for worker's rights to hazard pay and sick leave. Cries for reducing prison population gained urgency in light of the contagion. The protests and civil unrest ignited by the death of George Floyd saw sustained action against police brutality, and emphasized finding an end to racism, along with a surge of donations towards those causes. Rage isn't just for protests and marches, it can be felt in emails to representatives, petitions, and ballots. We can use our fury to keep the heat on those in power, and encourage others to join us. Even the outpouring of digital ways to connect online via concerts, performances, and group chats while we all sheltered in place built community support.

As individuals, we may not have the clout, connections, or resources to lobby the government. But the status quo of inequality is held in place by convincing us all to believe that change is impossible and unnecessary. Sure, the powerful are well funded and will always try to protect the broken systems that benefit them, but we must collectively resist returning to that system. We must see change as possible and necessary. A better, more equal society is feasible, and worth fighting for.

FURTHER INFORMATION AND ASSISTANCE

Federal Assistance

I f you are experiencing a low income, there may be federal assistance available to you. A great place to see what you qualify for is www.benefits.gov. If you're looking for immediate or emergency help, consider visiting or contacting your state's social services agency. Also note all services have income limits, and most require you to be a U.S. citizen or an eligible non-citizen.

- Unemployment Insurance
  - What it does: pays you money in the event of job loss.
  - Who qualifies: Those who have lost a job through no fault of their own, as well as state requirements.
  - Where to apply: 1-877-US2-JOBS or /www.careeronestop.org/LocalHelp/UnemploymentBenefits/unemployment-benefits.aspx

- Temporary Assistance for Needy Families (TANF)
  - What it does: Provide families with financial assistance and related support services (for a limited time). May offer non-cash benefits such as childcare and job training. If you receive TANF, you may be eligible to receive other benefits, like the Supplemental Nutrition Assistance Program (SNAP).
  - Who qualifies: Those who are pregnant or have a child under 19 and are low income or unemployed (additional qualifications vary state by state).

- ○ Where to apply: https://www.acf.hhs.gov/ofa/help; look up your state's phone number and local office.

- Medicaid

  - ○ What it does: Provides free or low-cost health coverage.

  - ○ Who qualifies: Low-income people, families and children, pregnant women, elderly people, and people with disabilities.

  - ○ Where to apply: 1-800-318-2596 or healthcare.gov or contact your state medicaid agency https://www.medicaid.gov/state-overviews/index.html

- Children's Health Insurance Program (CHIP)

  - ○ What it does: Offers free or low-cost medical and dental care to uninsured children (under 19).

  - ○ Who qualifies: Families with incomes above Medicaid's limit, but below their state's CHIP limit.

  - ○ Where to apply: 1-877-KIDS-NOW or healthcare.gov or find your state agency: https://www.insurekidsnow.gov/coverage/index.html

- Supplemental Nutrition Assistance Programs (known previously as food stamps)

  - ○ What it does: Provides you with a debit card, with provided funds, to purchase a defined set of grocery items for your household (for instance, no liquor, cleaning supplies, or hot foods). According to KFF, the national monthly average SNAP benefit per participant is $127.

  - ○ Who qualifies: People within 130% gross and 100% net percent of the poverty guideline (exceptions for those with household members who are elderly or disabled). Additionally, there is a work requirement, but there are exceptions for various instances: Those unable to work or participating in a drug treatment program, among others.

- ○ Where to apply: www.fns.usda.gov/snap/state-directory; look up your state's phone number and local office.

- Supplemental Security Income (SSI)

  - ○ What it does: Provides cash assistance.

  - ○ Who qualifies: adults and children with disabilities, and people over 65 with limited income.

  - ○ Where to apply: https://secure.ssa.gov/iClaim/dib or find your local office https://secure.ssa.gov/ICON/main.jsp

- Housing Assistance (also known as Section 8), and additional housing vouchers available through your local Public Housing Agency (PHA).

  - ○ What it does: Helps get people into affordable private or government owned rental housing. You would be free to choose any housing that meets the requirements of the program, and it is not limited to units located in subsidized housing projects. PHAs receive funds from the government and pay your landlord directly, leaving you to pay the remaining balance.

  - ○ Who qualifies: Low-income families and individuals, seniors, and people with disabilities. In general, the family's income may not exceed 50% of the median income for the county or metropolitan area in which the family chooses to live. By law, a PHA must provide 75 percent of its voucher to applicants whose incomes do not exceed 30 percent of the area median income. Median income levels are published by HUD and vary by location.

  - ○ More info: 1-800-955-2232; or contact your local PHA, listed here: https://www.hud.gov/program_offices/public_indian_housing/pha/contacts

REFERENCES

1. Adams, Susan. "Most Americans Are Unhappy At Work." Forbes. June 20, 2014. https://www.forbes.com/sites/susanadams/2014/06/20/most-americans-are-unhappy-at-work/#13d37fa3341a.

2. "Average Supplemental Nutrition Assistance Program (SNAP) Benefits Per Person." KFF. https://www.kff.org/other/state-indicator/avg-monthly-snap-benefits/?currentTimeframe=0&sortModel=%7B%22colId%22:%22Location%22,%22sort%22:%22asc%22%7D#

3. Berger, Rob. "Debt Snowball Versus Debt Avalanche: What The Academic Research Shows." Forbes. July 21, 2017. https://www.forbes.com/sites/robertberger/2017/07/20/debt-snowball-versus-debt-avalanche-what-the-academic-research-shows/#5c41ad0f1454.

4. "CFPB Rolls Back Restrictions on Payday Lenders." Marketplace. July 10, 2020. https://www.marketplace.org/2020/07/09/cfpb-rolls-back-restrictions-on-payday-lenders/.

5. DeSilver, Drew. "For Most Americans, Real Wages Have Barely Budged for Decades." Pew Research Center. May 30, 2020. https://www.pewresearch.org/fact-tank/2018/08/07/for-most-us-workers-real-wages-have-barely-budged-for-decades/.

6. "Elizabeth Gilbert on Distinguishing Between Hobbies, Jobs, Careers, & Vocation." *YouTube*, June 19, 2017, www.youtube.com/watch?v=0g7ARarFNnw.

7. Friedman, Zack. "78% Of Workers Live Paycheck To Paycheck." Forbes. January 11, 2019. https://www.forbes.com/sites/zackfriedman/2019/01/11/live-paycheck-to-paycheck-government-shutdown/#32175c244f10.

8. "Gender Pay Gap Statistics for 2020." PayScale. https://www.payscale.com/data/gender-pay-gap.

9. "How Many Credit Cards Should I Have?" The Ascent. https://www.fool.com/the-ascent/credit-cards/articles/how-many-credit-cards-does-the-average-person-have/.

10. "Illinois Paycheck Calculator." SmartAsset. https://smartasset.com/taxes/illinois-paycheck-calculator#v1DBdpBdGS.

11. Jackson, Tom. "How Payday Loans Work: Interest Rates, Fees and Costs." InCharge Debt Solutions. August 05, 2020. https://www.incharge.org/debt-relief/how-payday-loans-work/.

12. Klein, Alyson. "Poor Schools Found to Get Shortchanged; "Comparability of State and Local Expenditures Among Schools Within Districts: A Report From the Study of School-Level Expenditures"." Education Week 31, no. 13 (2011): 4.

13. Lexington Law. "2020 Average Credit Card Debt Statistics in the U.S." Lexington Law. July 20, 2020. https://www.lexingtonlaw.com/blog/loans/credit-card-debt-statistics.html.

14. Mitchell, Josh. "The Long Road to the Student Debt Crisis." The Wall Street Journal. June 07, 2019. https://www.wsj.com/articles/the-long-road-to-the-student-debt-crisis-11559923730?mod=article_inline.

15. Oliver, John, director. "Predatory Lending: Last Week Tonight with John Oliver." YouTube, August 10, 2014. www.youtube.com/watch?v=0g7ARarFNnw.

16. Oppenheimer, Daniel M ; Olivola, Christopher Y. "Feeling Good About Giving: The Benefits (and Costs) of Self-Interested Charitable Behavior." In The Science of Giving, 21-32. Psychology Press, 2011.

17. "Opportunity Insights." Opportunity Insights. https://opportunityinsights.org/.

18. "Out of Reach Report Graphics and Press Contact." National Low Income Housing Coalition. July 28, 2020. https://reports.nlihc.org/oor/report-graphics.

19. Parker, Will. "Rising Rents for Millennials Give Rise to a New Breed of Lender." The Wall Street Journal. May 13, 2019. https://www.wsj.com/articles/as-more-millennials-rent-more-startups-want-to-loan-to-them-11557739800?mod=article_inline.

20. Preprimary, Elementary, and Secondary Education - College Enrollment Rates - Indicator May (2020). https://nces.ed.gov/programs/coe/indicator_coi.asp.

21. Prins, Nomi. "The Rich Are Still Getting Richer." The Nation. February 26, 2019. https://www.thenation.com/article/inequality-wealth-rich-still-getting-richer/.

22. "Promoting Wellness for Better Behavioral and Physical Health." MFP. https://mfpcc.samhsa.gov/ENewsArticles/Article12b_2017.aspx.

23. "Report: Poor People's Campaign Moral Budget." Institute for Policy Studies. January 21, 2020. https://ips-dc.org/report-moral-budget-2/.

24. Ricardo Fuentes-Nieva. "Working for the Few." Oxfam International. September 22, 2014. https://www.oxfam.org/en/research/working-few.

25. Roth, Written By J.D., J.D. RothIn 2006, J.D. Roth, In 2006, and View All Posts by J.D. Roth. "Control Impulse Spending with the 30-day Rule." Get Rich Slowly. May 27, 2019. https://www.getrichslowly.org/control-impulse-spending-with-the-30-day-rule/.

26. The Condition of Education - Preprimary, Elementary, and Secondary Education - High School Completion - Public High School Graduation Rates - Indicator May (2020). https://nces.ed.gov/programs/coe/indicator_coi.asp.

27. "The Population of Poverty USA." Poverty Facts. https://www.povertyusa.org/facts.

28. "30 Million? 18 Million? How Many Americans Are out of Work Right Now?" Marketplace. August 07, 2020. https://www.marketplace.org/2020/08/06/how-many-americans-unemployed-right-now/.

29. Trent. "The Emotional Effects of Debt." The Simple Dollar. October 28, 2019. https://www.thesimpledollar.com/the-emotional-effects-of-debt/.

30. "2020 Poverty Guidelines." ASPE. January 21, 2020. https://aspe.hhs.gov/2020-poverty-guidelines.

31. "Wealth Inequality." Inequality.org. August 28, 2020. https://inequality.org/facts/wealth-inequality/#racial-wealth-divide.

32. "What Is a Good Credit Score?" Experian. September 02, 2020. https://www.experian.com/blogs/ask-experian/credit-education/score-basics/what-is-a-good-credit-score/.

ABOUT THE AUTHOR

Anna Jo Beck is an illustrator and magazine designer residing in Chicago, IL. Her work has been featured in The *New Yorker, Chicago Reader, Boston Dig*, and Netflix, as well as awarded by American Illustration. She is also authors the how-to zine series *Biff Boff Bam Sock* and is an organizer of the Chicago Zine Fest. Find more information on Anna and her work at annajobeck.com